Anabaptist Witness

A Global Anabaptist and Mennonite Dialogue on
Key Issues Facing the Church in Mission

VOLUME 1   OCTOBER 2014   ISSUE 1

Anabaptist Witness

A Global Anabaptist and Mennonite Dialogue on Key Issues Facing the Church in Mission

Co-Editors

Jamie Pitts, Anabaptist Mennonite Biblical Seminary
Jamie Ross, Mennonite Mission Network

Editorial Staff

VISUALS EDITOR SaeJin Lee
BOOK REVIEW EDITORS Steve Heinrichs & Isaac S. Villegas
COPY EDITOR Trisha Dale
MARKETING DIRECTOR Matthew J. Krabill
WEB EDITOR Gregory Rabus

Editorial Committee

Malinda Elizabeth Berry, Anabaptist Mennonite Biblical Seminary
Steve Heinrichs, Mennonite Church Canada Indigenous Relations
Matthew J. Krabill, Fuller Theological Seminary
SaeJin Lee, Anabaptist Mennonite Biblical Seminary
Gregory Rabus, church planter, conference of South German Mennonite Churches; Mannheim, Germany
Isaac S. Villegas, pastor of Chapel Hill Mennonite Fellowship; North Carolina, US

About

Anabaptist Witness is published twice a year (April and October). It is a publication of Anabaptist Mennonite Biblical Seminary, Mennonite Church Canada, and Mennonite Mission Network. The views expressed in *Anabaptist Witness* are those of the contributing writers and do not necessarily reflect the opinions of the partnering organizations.

Subscriptions, Additional Copies, and Change of Address

The annual subscription rate is $20 (US) plus shipping. Subscribers will receive an invoice to send with remittance to Anabaptist Mennonite Biblical Seminary. Single or additional copies of *Anabaptist Witness* are available for purchase through Amazon.com. Change of address or questions about purchasing the journal may be directed to the co-editors at the addresses below or by sending an e-mail to subscriptions@anabaptistwitness.org.

Editorial Correspondence

The co-editors make a public call for submissions for each issue of the journal, soliciting contributions that facilitate meaningful exchange among peoples from around the world, across professions, and from a variety of genres (sermons, photo-essays, interviews, biographies, poems, academic papers, etc.). For full details of the current call for submissions, visit www.anabaptistwitness.org. Questions or comments about the journal's print or online content may be directed to the co-editors:

Jamie Pitts   Jamie Ross
JPitts@AMBS.edu   JamieR@MMNWorld.net

Copyright

ISSN 2374-2534 (print)
ISSN 2374-2542 (online)

---

www.anabaptistwitness.org

Anabaptist Witness
Anabaptist Mennonite Biblical Seminary
3003 Benham Avenue
Elkhart, IN 46517 USA

*Website design by Studio Ace of Spade
*Print layout and cover design (title: *Connected*) by David Fast

Anabaptist Witness

A global Anabaptist and Mennonite dialogue on key issues facing the church in mission

| VOLUME 1 | OCTOBER 2014 | NUMBER 1 |

7 Editorial
Jamie Ross

ARTICLES

11 Formation théologique et identité anabaptiste: regards sur l'histoire mennonite
Neal Blough

27 A Vision for Global Mission amidst Shifting Realities
César García

37 Striving Towards Dependence: An Alternative Mennonite Anthropological Witness in Late Modernity
Jason Greig

61 The Hokkaido Confession of Faith and Mission in Japanese Context
Yoshihiro Kobayashi

69 The Shenandoah Confession: A Critical Introduction to the Next Generation
Evan Knappenberger

79 Evangelicalism, Anabaptism, and Being the Church in a Post-Christian Culture: An Interview with David Fitch
Carmen Andres

93 Dignity in Cross-Cultural Relationships: An Anabaptist Approach to Short-Term Missions
Robert Thiessen

97   A Re-Opened Ending: John 4:1-42 and the Church's Mission
     David Driedger

103 The Nothingness of the Church Under the Cross: Mission Without
     Colonialism
     Ry O. Siggelkow

121 Mennonites and Theological Education among Indigenous
     Churches in Ecuador: A Perspective from the Last Two Decades
     César Moya

135 Belong, Believe, Behave: Reflections on Church Planting in
     Germany
     Sharon Norton

141 Taking the Longer View
     Jeanne Jantzi

147 On the Way to Living Globally
     Walter Sawatsky

BOOK REVIEWS

167 Colin Godwin, *Baptizing, Gathering, and Sending*
     Reviewed by Chris Lenshyn

168 John Howard Yoder, *Theology of Mission*
     Reviewed by David Driedger

171 J. Denny Weaver, *The Nonviolent God*
     Reviewed by Chris Sabas

173 Willard M. Swartley, *Health, Healing, and the Church's Mission*
     Reviewed by April Yamasaki

175 Mark Amstutz, *Evangelicals and American Foreign Policy*
     Reviewed by Aaron Griffith

177 Kwok Pui-Lan, *Globalization, Gender, and Peacebuilding*
     Reviewed by Alain Epp Weaver

Editorial

Mission has been central to the Anabaptist movement from its beginning in the sixteenth century to its global presence today. This engagement in God's mission to and for the world continues to be facilitated by and stretched through dialogical missiological thinking and reflection. To these ends, Jamie Pitts and I as co-editors hope the relaunch of the journal *Anabaptist Witness*, previously known as *Mission Focus*, will drive the continuous evolution of the field of missiology, providing a place for a global Anabaptist and Mennonite dialogue on key issues facing the church in mission.

Mission Focus began in September of 1972 as a periodical edited by Wilbert Shenk at Mennonite Board of Missions. This brief mailer was sent out five times per year with a tagline that read, "For Mennonite mission leadership personnel. A new periodical." Shenk's first editorial named three reasons for the publication:

1. Controversy among Mennonites about the nature and purpose of mission;
2. The need for critical analysis of new missionary endeavors; and
3. The need to study the Bible, church, history, and current context to guide missionary work.

In 1979 the journal became a quarterly publication with the tagline, "*Mission Focus*: *from a believers church perspective*." In 1993, *Mission Focus* transitioned to an annual publication under the auspices of Anabaptist Mennonite Biblical Seminary. Walter Sawatsky became editor in 1997.

With Sawatsky's retirement in 2012, three agencies came together to discuss the renewal of *Mission Focus*, including Anabaptist Mennonite Biblical Seminary, Mennonite Church Canada, and Mennonite Mission Network. Jamie Pitts of AMBS and I were named co-editors in July of that year, tasked with the exciting work of leading this new partnership and the continuing transformation of *Mission Focus*. We are greatly assisted in our task by the six members of our editorial committee, which includes Malinda Berry, Steve Heinrichs, Matthew Krabill, SaeJin Lee, Gregory Rabus, and Isaac S. Villegas. We look forward to expanding global and organizational support and counsel in the years to come.

Sharing reflections, stories, and analysis of God's redeeming and transforming work around the world, *Anabaptist Witness* will be published twice each year, in April and October. All content is now peer-reviewed and will be available freely online, as well as in print through Amazon. We hope to engage pastors and lay people, mission agency staff and workers, professors and students. The co-editors welcome written and other artistic contributions from all corners of the church that will help us explore the intersections of Anabaptism and mission. Calls for contributions will be circulated regularly and widely.

As we hope for this to be a global resource, we are exploring possibilities for publishing in multiple languages and providing translations online as resources allow. The lead article in this first issue was written and published in French, by Neal Blough, and an English translation is available on our website. We also hope for Spanish translations of some of our articles to be available online in the coming months. Many different country and ethnic perspectives are represented in this first issue, as well as a broad range of perspectives from Anabaptists of various denominational and organizational backgrounds.

This first issue explores Anabaptist and Mennonite identities — how they have evolved and how they might help us live into our communities and the work God calls us to. As an example, Blough challenges us in his article to find creative ways to teach and sustain an Anabaptist theological identity, one that is made real through daily discipleship and both passed on to our congregations as well as shared with other Christians. It is this shared identity as Anabaptists, he contends, that might hold us together through interchurch schisms, and allow dialogue with each other and the broader church.

Articulating what it means to be Anabaptist in Japan, Yoshihiro Kobayashi documents the motivations for writing the Hokkaido Confession of Faith and its implications for being faithful to the good news of Jesus Christ. He presents the confession as both a contextualization of what it means to be Anabaptist in Japan, and as a call to fellow Christians around the world to take seriously Jesus' witness of radical inclusivity. These dynamics of articulating and contextualizing faith are continued in Evan Knappenberger's article, in which he shares the newly released Shenandoah Confession. This confession was written by several young Anabaptists who participated in the Occupy Wall Street movement and were then challenged at the Intercollegiate Peace Meeting at Eastern Mennonite University to articulate their faith together.

While we explore new mission movements and the work of a younger generation, we intend to engage the writings and ministries of those who came before us. You will notice that there are several references in this issue to John Howard Yoder (1927–97), a Mennonite theologian whose work has been widely influential in Anabaptist and Mennonite missiology. We as co-editors affirm the need for critical scholarship on Yoder's writings that takes account of his grievous sexual misconduct. As stated in our Author Guidelines (http://anabaptistwitness.org/guidelines/), we encourage the examination of normative theological claims in light of the lives of the persons or communities making them. We invite readers and contributors to help us discern the shape of responsible research and reflection on mission in the coming issues of *Anabaptist Witness*.

As missiology is cross-disciplinary in nature, this issue includes sermons, reflections on church planting, book reviews, and academic articles on theological education, theology, and history. This issue calls us to identify what our communities mean when we claim our Anabaptist identities. Furthermore, as in Ry O. Siggelkow's article, it challenges us to go beyond reflection to renewed thinking that results in changed behavior, "living in expectancy of the coming of God's kingdom."

However you came across this renewed publication, I am glad it is in your hands or on your computer screen. Let us learn together as Anabaptists what it means to engage God's mission and work in this world. Be sure to visit our website (anabaptistwitness.org) to read exclusive online content, sign up for emails, find calls for contributions, and see how you might further engage this resource.

Welcome to *Anabaptist Witness*.

Jamie Ross, Co-Editor

Formation théologique et identité anabaptiste:

regards sur l'histoire mennonite[1]

NEAL BLOUGH[2]

Abstract: This article examines the relationship between a "wounded" Mennonite identity, theological education, and mission in relation to questions being asked among members of the Mennonite Francophone Network today. From its sixteenth-century beginnings, Anabaptism bore the wounds of rejection, persecution, and marginalization. In some cases this led to a Mennonite mentality of separation and legalism. Nineteenth-century efforts to overcome the "wounds of sectarianism" and "spiritual drought" led to openness to Pietism and Evangelical Protestantism. In France, Switzerland, and North America, nineteenth-century beginnings of theological education were tied to renewal movements and interest in mission as a way of renewing an often ethnic Mennonite identity prone to formalism. This combination, plus the mission movement's insistence on Protestant unity, led to a downplaying of a more specifically "Anabaptist" theological identity when new churches were born in Congo or Burkina Faso. Another means for renewing Mennonite identity has been through a return to sixteenth-century historical origins, which in the last half century has produced fruits in terms of a more Anabaptist missiology and a world-wide identity promoted by Mennonite World Conference. French-speaking Mennonites in Canada, Europe, and Africa are searching for theological education that will form leaders and congregations in a more positive Anabaptist identity, while at the same time assuming a conscious role in the larger context of a worldwide Christian family still too often divided.

---

1 Find an English translation of this article at http://anabaptistwitness.org/journal_entry/theological-education-and-anabaptist-identity-perspectives-from-mennonite-history/.

2 *Neal Blough est directeur Centre Mennonite de Paris, professeur d'histoire de l'Eglise à la Faculté Libre de Théologie Evangélique de Vaux sur Seine, et il enseigne aussi au CEFOR/ Bienenberg (Suisse) et à l'Institut Catholique de Paris. Il est co-directeur de la série "Perspectives anabaptistes" publiée aux Editions Excelsis.*
Présentation donnée à la Consultation sur la Formation théologique du Réseau mennonite francophone à Kinshasa, février 2014.

Le développement du réseau mennonite francophone reflète des dévelop-
pements récents dans l'histoire mennonite. L'auteur de ces lignes est né
en 1950. Depuis, le monde mennonite francophone a beaucoup évolué.
En 1950, la France se relevait de la Deuxième Guerre Mondiale qui l'avait
profondément touchée. À ce moment là, il y avait deux groupements structurés
d'églises mennonites. Le plus grand, le groupe alsacien, était encore largement
germanophone. Aujourd'hui, il n'y a qu'une association mennonite en France
et les cultes se font tous en français, une transition importante, à la fois linguis-
tique et culturelle[3].

L'association mennonite suisse (Conférence Mennonite Suisse) se compose
d'assemblées germanophones et francophones, et son journal mensuel Perspective est bilingue. La disparition d'écoles primaires mennonites dans le Jura fait
désormais du français la première langue dans plusieurs communautés mennonites suisses. Ainsi, dans les deux pays européens où les mennonites parlent
le français, le nombre d'assemblées reste très petit, autour d'une quarantaine[4].
En 1950, il n'y a pas encore d'Église mennonite au Québec. L'Église mennonite
du Canada commence à implanter des églises au Québec en 1957 et les Frères
mennonites en 1963, avec des missionnaires ayant travaillé au Congo. Il existe
une communauté mennonite québécoise aujourd'hui, mais elle est extrêmement
petite[5].

L'année 1950 marque quarante ans d'activité missionnaire au Congo (pendant lesquelles des liens sont créés avec les églises anglophones d'Amérique du
Nord) qui donne naissance à l'une des communautés mennonites les plus importantes au monde. C'est là que se trouve le plus grand nombre de mennonites
parlant le français, bien que ce soit très souvent leur deuxième ou troisième

---

3 Jean Séguy, *Les Assemblées anabaptistes-mennonites de France*, Paris, Mouton,
1977 ; N. Blough, A. Hoekema et H. Jecker, (dir.), *Foi et Tradition à l'Épreuve*, Histoire
générale des Mennonites dans le Monde, II. L'Europe, Editions Excelsis, collection
Perspectives anabaptistes, 2012, p. 187-200 ; N. Blough, « Harold Bender, 'La Vision
anabaptiste' et les Mennonites de France », *Bulletin de la Société d'Histoire du Protestantisme français*, janvier-mars 2002, p. 151-177.

4 Blough, Hoekema et Jecker, (dir.), *Foi et Tradition à l'Épreuve*, p. 169-186.

5 Robert Martin-Koop, « Quebec (Canada) » [en ligne], *Global Anabaptist Mennonite Encyclopedia Online*, 1990, http://gameo.org/index.php?title=Quebec_(Canada)&oldid=114360, consulté le 5 juin 2014 ;

*Jean Raymond Théorêt, « Quebec Conference of Mennonite Brethren Churches » [en
ligne], Global Anabaptist Mennonite Encyclopedia Online, August 2011, http://gameo.org/
index.php?title=Quebec_Conference_of_Mennonite_Brethren_Churches&oldid=77108, consulté le 5 june 2014.*

langue[6].

En ce qui concerne le Burkina Faso, les débuts de l'Église mennonite datent de 1983[7].

Bien que la Conférence Mennonite Mondiale ait été créée en 1925, ce n'est que depuis quelques décennies que des liens se tissent de manière plus étroite entre les mennonites du monde entier, et seulement depuis une petite quinzaine d'années que les mennonites francophones cherchent délibérément à établir des liens entre eux via le Réseau mennonite francophone[8]. La tenue d'une Consultation mennonite francophone internationale, qui ne pouvait guère se concevoir en 1950, est devenue réalité en février 2014, à Kinshasa.

Pour situer le propos de cet article, qui concerne le lien entre « formation théologique » et « identité anabaptiste », commençons par citer l'un des participants au colloque de Kinshasa, Siaka Traoré, qui dans sa postface à *Rythmes anabaptistes en Afrique*, constate la relation entre identité théologique et héritage missionnaire.

> […] Au début, les missions mennonites n'ont pas mis un accent particulier sur l'identité mennonite.
>
> À défaut de connaître leur identité, nombreuses sont les Églises qui se sont conformées aux Églises dominantes dans leur contexte. Elles embrassent la théologie ou la doctrine dominante dans le pays[9].

Lors de plusieurs déplacements à Kinshasa, j'ai entendu cette même remarque de plusieurs pasteurs mennonites congolais : « Les missions ont fondé nos églises sans nous dire que nous étions mennonites ». Bien qu'il y ait un élément de vérité important, cette remarque pourrait laisser entendre que la question d'identité anabaptiste-mennonite n'est un problème qu'en Afrique, ou un problème ayant son origine dans la mission. Cependant, comme nous le verrons, il n'y a pas qu'en Afrique que se pose cette question. Le phénomène constaté par Siaka Traoré fait partie de l'histoire mennonite depuis ses origines.

La question de l'identité théologique traverse l'histoire mennonite comme elle traverse l'histoire de toute famille chrétienne. Dans les paragraphes qui suivent, nous proposons de développer un regard comparatif sur l'histoire men-

---

6 *Rythmes anabaptistes en Afrique*, Collectif, Histoire générale des Mennonites dans le Monde, I. L'Afrique, Editions Excelsis, collection Perspectives anabaptistes, 2012, p. 49-102.

7 Ibid., p. 278-280.

8 Réseau mennonite francophone, « Vivre l'Église au-delà des Frontières », *Dossiers de Christ Seul*, Éditions Mennonites, N° 1, 2012.

9 *Rythmes anabaptistes en Afrique*, p. 281.

nonite de plusieurs lieux représentés à cette consultation. Cette approche traite de l'identité théologique et son lien avec la formation théologique, mais aussi avec la pratique missionnaire insérée dans le contexte chrétien plus large que mennonite : identité mennonite, formation théologique, mission et relations avec d'autres familles chrétiennes.

Remarques sur les origines anabaptistes-mennonites et l'identité théologique

Notre identité est complexe et comporte souvent des blessures. Des éléments historiques marquent fortement l'identité des pays présents à cette consultation : le colonialisme, l'esclavage, l'injustice économique entre le Nord et le Sud et la mission. Ces éléments font partie — consciemment ou non — de notre identité, et nous devons gérer ces blessures et en guérir. En fait, nous portons ensemble la blessure profonde du mal, comme nous portons l'espérance de l'Évangile de la réconciliation et de la guérison du mal.

Sur le plan historique, l'identité mennonite elle-même est empreinte de blessures. Elle s'est construite à partir d'un rejet profond de la part d'autres chrétiens dès ses origines, un rejet produisant une identité minoritaire, pas toujours sûre d'elle-même et tiraillée entre le désir de rester fidèle aux éléments clés de ses origines et la lassitude d'être différente et considérée comme sectaire et méprisable. Les blessures de cette identité mennonite complexe sont ressenties, d'une manière ou d'une autre, par la plupart des Églises représentées ici.

Depuis ses origines, les anabaptistes, issus de la théologie chrétienne, ont gardé bon nombre de points commun avec elle. Ses spécificités concernent la conception de l'Église et un accent fort sur la vie chrétienne comme « suivance » de Jésus-Christ. Parmi les réformateurs du xvie siècle, seuls les anabaptistes ont une pratique missionnaire, due à leur théologie du baptême et leur ecclésiologie. Cependant, par la force des circonstances, cet élan missionnaire a plus ou moins disparu.

Dans les débuts de l'anabaptisme, la formation théologique n'est pas dénigrée. Parmi les premiers anabaptistes se trouvent des personnes ayant étudié à l'université (Conrad Grebel, Felix Mantz, Balthasar Hubmaier), d'anciens prêtres formés dans l'Église catholique (Georges Blaurock, Michaël Sattler, Menno Simons), ou des professionnels laïcs ayant un haut niveau de connaissances théologiques (Pilgram Marpeck). Les réformateurs du xvie siècle comprennent le lien fondamental entre formation et identité théologique, car la Réforme marque une période de renouveau de la formation théologique, à la fois dans le monde protestant et catholique[10]. Jusque très récemment[11], les mouvements de réforme, de renouveau ou de réveil s'accompagnaient d'une conscience aigue de la nécessité de la formation théologique, reconnaissant que celle-ci est nécessaire pour créer, maintenir et transmettre l'identité théologique et ecclésiale.

Cependant, une conséquence importante de la blessure du rejet, de la persécution et de la marginalisation des mouvements anabaptistes est la suivante : après le milieu du xvie siècle, les mennonites d'Europe n'ont plus de pasteurs ou de prédicateurs formés autrement que par l'étude de la Bible, la prédication et l'expérience pastorale. L'identité théologique des assemblées persécutées et dispersées se transmet et s'entretient par le culte, la prédication, le chant, la lecture de la Bible et du *Miroir des Martyrs*[12], ainsi que par la spiritualité individuelle et communautaire.

Ainsi, à partir de la fin du xvie siècle, le contexte européen a produit un anabaptisme « meurtri » et dispersé, ayant des conducteurs spirituels sans formation théologique, et même, généralement, sans aucune formation. Le fait que leurs adversaires protestants ou catholiques aient des connaissances théologiques a aussi pu produire des réactions de rejet à l'égard de la formation : « C'est à l'université et dans les séminaires qu'on apprend la mauvaise théologie qui a entraîné notre persécution, donc il faut éviter de se former théologiquement. » La seule exception sera l'anabaptisme néerlandais : les mennonites sont mieux tolérés aux Pays-Bas et mettent en place un séminaire de théologie en 1735[13]. Cependant, cela reflète déjà une assimilation culturelle qui laisse rapi-

---

10 À ce propos, voir notre article « Perspectives historiques sur la formation théologique protestante et évangélique, du XVIe au XXe siècle », *Théologie évangélique*, 11 (2012), p. 23-32.

11 Certaines formes de protestantisme américain du xvie siècle commencent à dénigrer la formation théologique comme élitiste, et beaucoup de formes du mouvement charismatique affirmeraient qu'une expérience directe de l'Esprit est beaucoup plus importante que toute formation.

12 Les anabaptistes ont raconté et rédigé l'histoire de leurs martyrs, la version la plus utilisée étant le Martelaersspiel (Miroir des martyrs) qui date de 1660 et a 1290 pages. Cet ouvrage a été traduit d'abord en allemand et ensuite en anglais. Une sélection de ces récits se trouve dans John S. Oyer & Robert S. Kreider, *Miroir des Martyrs. Histoires d'Anabaptistes ayant donné leur Vie pour leur Foi au XVIe siècle*, Editions Excelsis, collection *Perspectives Anabaptistes*, 2003.

13 Blough, Hoekema et Jecker, (dir.), *Foi et Tradition à l'Épreuve*, p. 64.

dement de côté des éléments importants de l'identité anabaptiste[14].

Le cas de la France peut servir d'exemple de ce qui pouvait se passer ailleurs en Europe. Les communautés anabaptistes présentes dans l'est du pays[15] vivent à l'écart, avec des anciens et des prédicateurs formés par l'expérience à l'intérieur de la communauté. Le schisme amish (1693) est largement suivi par les anabaptistes français, ce qui renforce le caractère « séparé » et « à part » de leur identité. Tout en connaissant les tentations du légalisme et de l'autoritarisme (chez les anciens), au XVIIe et le XVIIIe siècle, l'anabaptisme franco-alsacien maintient cependant plusieurs aspects de l'identité théologique anabaptiste, dont le refus de la violence. Avec la Révolution française et la période napoléonienne, l'État français commence à demander aux anabaptistes de servir dans l'armée. En France et ailleurs, les mennonites qui tiennent à la non-violence ou à d'autres spécificités anabaptistes, choisissent souvent d'émigrer vers l'Amérique du Nord. En grande partie à cause de l'émigration, l'anabaptisme français est sur le point de disparaître au début du XXe siècle[16] et les églises mennonites européennes sont affaiblies.

Piétisme, missions et identité mennonite

Le XIXe siècle est une période-clé pour comprendre le contexte mennonite d'aujourd'hui. C'est le moment où l'anabaptisme est très influencé par le piétisme évangélique, ce qui a comme conséquence l'entrée des mennonites dans le grand mouvement missionnaire protestant qui date de la fin du XVIIIe siècle et du début du XIXe[17].

Chez les mennonites français, suisses, allemands du Sud, russes et désormais nord-américains[18], la vie à l'écart, le caractère ethnique des communautés et le manque de responsables formés produisent assez souvent une vie d'église desséchée sinon légaliste. En Europe, l'émigration en Amérique contribue aussi à diminuer le nombre de responsables des communautés anabaptistes, et en outre, à s'éloigner de certains aspects de l'identité théologique anabaptiste des églises.

---

14 « À partir de 1780, la tradition de la paix qui existait chez les mennonites néerlandais disparut quasiment, du moins parmi la partie libérale qui dominait. » (Blough, Hoekema et Jecker, (dir.), *Foi et Tradition à l'Épreuve*, p. 77)

15 Souvent dans des territoires encore germanophones.

16 Pour les détails, voir Jean Séguy, *Les Assemblées anabaptistes-mennonites de France*.

17 L'influence du piétisme sur l'anabaptisme ne commence pas au XIXe siècle, mais c'est à ce moment-là que la mission devient un élément important de cette influence.

18 Le XIXe siècle mennonite nord-américain connait beaucoup de diversité et beaucoup de schismes. (Blough, Hoekema et Jecker, (dir.), *Foi et Tradition*, p. 260).

Dans beaucoup de cas, une soif de vie spirituelle plus profonde tout à fait compréhensible pousse les mennonites vers les mouvements de réveil piétiste. Pour certains, la blessure identitaire est très profonde. Pour de nombreuses personnes, le « mennonitisme » n'est qu'une religion familiale et « formaliste ». En Russie, cela produit par exemple un schisme important qui donne naissance à l'Église des « Frères mennonites » en 1860[19]. Mais il n'y a pas qu'en Russie que se produisent de tels changements.

> Les mouvements de Réveil du XIXe et du début du XXe siècle furent plus que des événements passagers. Ils provoquèrent des changements décisifs dans la vie spirituelle des assemblées mennonites suisses (mais aussi françaises, allemandes et nord américaines)[20].

À partir de ce moment-là, les mennonites d'Europe (sauf aux Pays-Bas et en Allemagne du Nord) commencent à envoyer des prédicateurs dans les écoles bibliques piétistes. La participation à une formation théologique institutionnalisée commence à voir le jour, mais dans ces contextes non-mennonites.

> Les centres de formations, tels que l'institut biblique de St. Chrischona près de Bâle, ont non seulement joué un rôle central dans la formation de générations de prédicateurs mennonites de Suisse, d'Alsace, du sud de l'Allemagne et du sud de la Russie, mais ils contribuèrent également à instaurer une certaine harmonie sur le plan théologique[21].

Mission et formation théologique

Nous venons de le constater : les mennonites européens et nord-américains du XIXe siècle ont des débats importants et difficiles sur l'identité théologique de leurs communautés. Aux Pays-Bas et en Allemagne du Nord, où les assemblées sont plus intégrées dans la société et le monde urbain, les mennonites sont tiraillés entre le protestantisme libéral et le piétisme, mais penchent vers la théologie libérale. Les pasteurs sont formés au séminaire d'Amsterdam. En revanche, en Suisse, en France, en Allemagne du Sud et en Russie, les communautés anabaptistes teintées de sectarisme et de légalisme regardent vers le piétisme pour en sortir. En Amérique du Nord, la réalité est multiple, allant de théologies anabaptistes plutôt séparatistes et conservatrices (par exemple les amish) à celles exprimant le désir d'une intégration plus nette dans le contexte du protestantisme évangélique américain. Contrairement aux Pays-Bas, la plupart des assemblées que nous venons de mentionner se trouvent en milieu rural.

---

19 Ibid., Hoekema et Jecker, (dir.), *Foi et Tradition*, p. 214.

20 Ibid., Hoekema et Jecker, (dir.), *Foi et Tradition*, p. 173. (C'est nous qui ajoutons la parenthèse à la fin de la citation).

21 Ibid., Hoekema et Jecker, (dir.), *Foi et Tradition*, p. 173.

Le mouvement vers le piétisme reflète une critique de l'état des assemblées et un désir de mieux intégrer la culture ambiante européenne ou américaine. Autrement dit, l'identité mennonite telle qu'elle est vécue et comprise rencontre des critiques importantes.

C'est pendant cette période que les mennonites européens commencent à envoyer des prédicateurs à St. Chrischona, une école piétiste (évangélique). Aux États-Unis d'Amérique, une école pour former des prédicateurs mennonites est fondée à Wadsworth (Ohio) en 1868, avec un programme de niveau secondaire[22]. En Europe et en Amérique du Nord, ce mouvement vers le piétisme est en même temps un mouvement vers la mission. Pour ceux qui voudraient « réveiller » les assemblées mennonites, la mission semble être une clé importante. Le mouvement missionnaire protestant, fruit du renouveau piétiste, date de la fin du XVIIIe/début du XIXe siècle. Les mennonites vont y participer, mais un peu plus tard que les autres. Les premiers missionnaires mennonites sont néerlandais, et sont influencés, eux aussi, par le piétisme. Ils commencent d'abord à collaborer avec une mission baptiste, puis fondent leur propre société missionnaire mennonite en 1847 pour travailler en Indonésie[23]. Cette mission néerlandaise est soutenue par des mennonites allemands, russes, alsaciens, suisses et même nord-américains.

Les mennonites nord-américains se joignent ensuite au mouvement missionnaire. Comme en Europe, les mennonites nord-américains qui s'intéressent à la mission souhaitent apporter « une vie nouvelle » dans leurs assemblées. D'ailleurs, le premier missionnaire mennonite américain (envoyé vers les amérindiens) est un immigré mennonite d'Allemagne qui a fait l'école de Wadsworth[24], où l'on apprend à quitter le « formalisme mennonite et à travailler de manière intelligente et agressive pour le Maître »[25]. Ainsi les débuts de la formation théologique pour les mennonites européens et américains touchés

---

22 Harold S. Bender et Erland Waltner, « Seminaries » [en ligne], *Global Anabaptist Mennononite Encyclopedia Online*, 1989, http://gameo.org/index.php?title=Seminaries, consulté le 2 septembre 2014.

23 Blough, Hoekema et Jecker, (dir.), *Foi et Tradition à l'Épreuve*, p. 80-82.

24 « The earliest Mennonite missionaries saw their work as sparking new life in Mennonite communities at home. Samuel (S.S.) Haury was a Wadsworth trained, south German immigrant who in 1880 became the first American Mennonite to go out in mission work among culturally different people. Through mission Haury hoped to 'bring new life and rejuvenation to the empty or hollow formalities are declining churches are guilty of' ». James C. Juhnke, *Vision, Doctrine, War. Mennonite Identity and Organization in America 1890-1930*, Herald Press, 1989, p. 141.

25 Ibid., *Vision, Doctrine, War*, p. 133.

par le piétisme, sont fortement liés à l'intérêt pour la mission.

Selon l'historien et missiologue mennonite Wilbert Shenk, le premier siècle d'activité missionnaire mennonite européen et nord-américain est profondément marqué par le monde piétiste (ou évangélique)[26], d'où viennent la motivation et l'énergie. En outre, les mennonites sont souvent parmi les derniers arrivés sur « le champs de mission », devenant ainsi des partenaires « mineurs ». Ne trouvant ni énergie ou vision missionnaire dans leur propre expérience mennonite, ils tirent leur missiologie et leur stratégie du monde évangélique.

La première mission mennonite au Congo va dans ce sens. Deux groupes mennonites, ayant des racines alsaciennes récentes, commencent un travail missionnaire au Kasaï vers 1911-12[27]. N'ayant pas de personne compétente dans leurs propres rangs, la « *Congo Inland Mission* » choisit des évangéliques non-mennonites pour formuler leur vision et trouver du personnel[28].

Toujours selon W. Shenk, de cette première période d'activité missionnaire jusque vers 1950, il n'existe pas de réflexion missiologique spécifiquement anabaptiste. Même s'il commence à y avoir des missionnaires formés dans la perspective de la « vision anabaptiste » vers 1950, la période d'expansion missionnaire mennonite après-guerre, jusque vers 1965 est, selon W. Shenk, essentiellement « évangélique ».

Notre démarche consiste à décrire, non à juger. Cette influence piétiste a probablement permis aux mennonites suisses et français de survivre. En outre, le mouvement missionnaire a une préoccupation importante, l'unité, car depuis ses origines, le protestantisme est une réalité fractionnée et divisée. La plupart des églises protestantes ou évangéliques sont issues de schismes douloureux, dont la première rupture avec l'Église catholique au XVIe siècle. Les premiers efforts vers l'unité protestante viennent de mouvements comme l'Alliance Évangélique, fondée à Londres en 1846, et plus tard, du mouvement missionnaire occidental qui commence à travailler avec d'autres et à tenir des conférences internationales vers la fin du XIXe siècle. Lors d'une conférence missionnaire importante à Édimbourg en 1910, les représentants chinois ont interpellé les protestants occidentaux en posant la question de savoir pourquoi les divisions historiques du protestantisme sont exportées ailleurs dans le monde. Pourquoi les Chinois et les Africains doivent-ils s'appeler luthériens, réformés, anglicans

---

26 Pour les paragraphes qui suivent, je me base sur W.R. Shenk, *By Faith They Went Out. Mennonite Missions 1850-1899*, Elkhart, Institute of Mennonite Studies, 2000, surtout le chapitre 2 : « Mennonites and the Emerging Evangelical Network," p. 29-49.

27 Une « anticipation » du réseau francophone à venir un siècle plus tard ?

28 Juhnke, *Vision, Doctrine, War*, p. 150.

ou méthodistes ? Pourquoi le travail missionnaire ne peut-il pas être une œuvre commune ? Beaucoup voient d'ailleurs dans cette association de 1910 un facteur important contribuant à la naissance du Conseil Œcuménique des Églises quelques décennies plus tard[29].

Cette dynamique d'unité protestante est à l'œuvre très tôt au Congo, car

[…] suite à une association missionnaire internationale en 1910 à Édimbourg, (Écosse), les missions protestantes œuvrant au Congo constituèrent un comité de continuation qui devint par la suite le Conseil protestant au Congo (CPC) en 1924[30].

De plus, le favoritisme du gouvernement belge envers les missions catholiques suscite des tensions importantes sur le plan missionnaire.

Cette tension (entre protestants et catholiques), peut-être plus que tout autre facteur, poussa les mennonites et les autres protestants à travailler en vue d'une unité protestante durant cette période, ce qui eut pour conséquence inévitable de souligner ce qu'ils avaient en commun, plutôt que de mettre l'accent sur leurs caractéristiques distinctives[31].

Ainsi, au moins deux facteurs importants expliquent le « manque » d'identité mennonite dans le travail missionnaire : 1) l'insertion des mennonites européens et nord-américains dans le mouvement missionnaire issu du renouveau piétiste et évangélique et, 2) l'importance donnée par ce mouvement missionnaire à l'unité protestante.

Le fait que les missions n'aient pas transmis « d'identité mennonite » claire aux églises congolaises, reflète des problèmes d'identité théologique se posant chez les mennonites nord- américains et européens. Ainsi, la question d'identité est commune à tous les mennonites et ne concerne pas uniquement les Congolais ou les Burkinabés.

Histoire anabaptiste et identité

Le piétisme et l'engagement missionnaire sont des manières de renouveler l'identité mennonite européenne et américaine en crise, mais d'autres personnes (et parfois les mêmes) se tournent vers l'histoire anabaptiste et la vision théologique des origines pour redonner vie à des assemblées marquées par l'ethnicité et le séparatisme d'un côté, et le désir d'assimilation culturelle de l'autre. Les mennonites ont toujours fait référence à leur histoire pour maintenir leur identité ; il suffit de constater l'importance du *Miroir des Martyrs* et d'autres

---

29 Voir la revue *Perspectives missionnaires* 2010/2 – N° 60, Dossier Édimbourg – Cape Town 2010.

30 *Rythmes anabaptistes*, p. 55.

31 Ibid., p. 63.

écrits tout au long des siècles. Cependant, vers la fin du xixe siècle (donc la période pendant laquelle certains mennonites se tournent vers le piétisme et l'engagement missionnaire), les historiens de l'Europe commencent à porter un regard beaucoup plus positif sur les mouvements anabaptistes du xvie siècle[32]. C'est peut-être le début de la guérison de la blessure identitaire, car d'autres aussi commencent à affirmer que la tradition anabaptiste mérite d'être mieux considérée. Certains historiens mennonites allemands relaient ce renouveau historiographique dans leurs assemblées dans l'espoir de revitaliser des églises qui se trouvent soit emprisonnées dans un traditionalisme porté par l'ethnicité, soit tentées de devenir simplement de bons protestants libéraux ou évangéliques. Quelques jeunes mennonites américains, dont Harold Bender, viennent en Europe pour apprendre de ce renouveau historiographique[33].

C'est aussi l'époque d'un fort nationalisme en Europe et en Amérique du Nord. Dans ces pays, les mennonites commencent à se sentir allemands, néerlandais, français, suisses, canadiens ou américains. Ce nationalisme produit bientôt des ravages inimaginables pendant les deux guerres mondiales, et la plupart des mennonites européens cèdent aux sirènes de la guerre, c'est-à-dire aux idéologies et aux théologies dominantes de l'époque. Ni l'adaptation libérale des mennonites néerlandais, ni l'adaptation piétiste des Français, Suisses ou Allemands n'a permis de résister au nationalisme ou aux efforts de guerre.

Les circonstances jouent toujours un rôle important dans l'élaboration d'une identité. En missiologie, ce processus est appelé « contextualisation ». Le choc de la Deuxième Guerre Mondiale, la menace des armes atomiques et la nouvelle guerre froide posent la question de la paix et de la non-violence avec une nouvelle urgence. Les mennonites européens ne viennent-ils pas de passer par des horreurs indescriptibles ? Et dans un contexte américain où l'objection de conscience et le service civil sont possibles, pourquoi presque la moitié des hommes mennonites ne le choisissent-ils pas ? Des mennonites ne viennent-ils pas de s'engager dans les armées française, allemande, russe, américaine et canadienne ? Les chrétiens occidentaux du xxe siècle n'ont-ils pas largement échoué dans leur tâche d'être « sel et lumière du monde » et « artisans de paix » ?

Le « retour à l'histoire anabaptiste » s'est poursuivi dans les années d'après-guerre et a largement contribué à la réflexion sur la non-violence à partir des années 1950. Le renouveau de l'historiographie mennonite a commencé en

32 Voir notre *Mennonites d'hier et d'aujourd'hui*, Éditions Mennonites, 2009, p. 49-51.

33 Voir Jean Séguy, « La 'Vision anabaptiste' de Harold S. Bender à nos Jours », *Bulletin de la Société de l'Histoire du Protestantisme Français*, 148 (2002), p. 119-150.

Europe. Cependant, suite aux dévastations provoquées par les deux guerres mondiales et grâce au tissu institutionnel et universitaire mennonite nord-américain, le travail historique se fait en grande majorité en Amérique du Nord. Plusieurs éléments sont les « porteurs institutionnels » de ce renouveau théologique : les lieux de formation, le MCC et, désormais, les organisations missionnaires.

Formation théologique et identité (mission et histoire se rencontrent enfin)

À partir du début du xxᵉ siècle, la vie des mennonites européens est compliquée par l'affaiblissement résultant de l'émigration vers l'Amérique du Nord et par les destructions causées par les deux guerres mondiales. Aujourd'hui, les mennonites d'Europe représentent 4% de la population mennonite mondiale. Il y a un siècle, ils en constituaient la moitié. C'est différent en Amérique du Nord, continent qui a bénéficié de l'immigration mennonite et qui n'a pas connu de manière directe les effets des guerres. C'est aussi la période de l'institutionnalisation mennonite américaine, car entre 1890 et 1930 vont naître des écoles primaires et secondaires et universitaires, des maisons d'édition, des hôpitaux et des maisons de retraite mennonites. Les premières missions se structurent en organisations missionnaires, et la naissance du MCC (travail de collaboration américano-européen) a un impact important dans la vie des assemblées[34].

En dépit de ces nouvelles institutions, les mennonites nord-américains restent quelque peu réticents devant une formation théologique trop poussée. Comme en Alsace, en Allemagne du Sud ou en Suisse, on souhaite plutôt des prédicateurs laïcs et, si formation il y a, elle est souvent limitée à ce qu'on peut recevoir dans un institut biblique ou dans les départements bibliques des « collèges » mennonites[35]. Cependant, la mise en place d'études de niveau universitaire dans des écoles mennonites amène le début d'un changement sociologique important : les mennonites nord-américains commencent à quitter les fermes pour adopter d'autres métiers. Cette évolution favorise la mise en place d'écoles bibliques et de facultés de théologie, à l'image d'autres institutions dénominationnelles[36]. Les assemblées commencent à constater les bienfaits d'avoir des pasteurs mieux formés, tout en voulant qu'ils acquièrent une perspective

---

34 Juhnke, *Vision, Doctrine, War*, p. 29.

35 « Collège » dans le contexte nord-américain est une école qui attribue la licence (Bachelor's Degree).

36 Liste non exhaustive : Bluffton (Witmarsum Theological Seminary), 1914 ; Goshen Bible School (1933-1946) ; Eastern Mennonite Bible School, 1938 ; Mennonite Brethren Bible College (Winnipeg) 1944 ;

théologique anabaptiste. Les facultés de théologie sont justement les lieux de transmission d'une théologie plus spécifiquement anabaptiste qui fait son chemin vers les assemblées, les institutions et les organisations missionnaires. En fait, le « retour à l'histoire anabaptiste » et la mise en place de lieux de formation universitaires ont joué un rôle fondamental dans le renouveau de l'identité mennonite. J'ai personnellement bénéficié de ce renouveau identitaire pendant mes années d'études ; mais pour un historien, le phénomène paraît très récent. C'est surtout pendant la deuxième moitié du XXᵉ siècle que ces changements ont lieu, autrement dit, pendant la courte période de ma vie.

En Europe, les mennonites sont trop peu nombreux pour créer un tel réseau institutionnel. Des mennonites germanophones continuent à fréquenter l'école de St. Chrischona, ou des facultés de théologie des Églises officielles, tandis que des mennonites francophones commencent à fréquenter l'Institut biblique de Nogent, fondé en 1921. Une école biblique mennonite européenne (francophone et germanophone) est fondée en 1950 au Bienenberg. La section francophone se dénomme le Centre de Formation et de Rencontre (CEFOR). La Faculté Libre de Théologie Évangélique de Vaux-sur-Seine (près de Paris) est fondée en 1965, avec le soutien de mennonites français ; plusieurs pasteurs ou enseignants mennonites contemporains y ont fait leurs études.

Au Congo, on constate une évolution semblable : une École biblique inter-mennonite a été fondée à Kajiji en 1963. Selon Eric Kumedisa :

> [...] L'école de théologie de Kajiji joua un rôle essentiel dans la formation de dirigeants mieux qualifiés pour les Églises mennonites, en renforçant un esprit de coopération entre les mennonites, et en créant un fort sentiment d'unité parmi les étudiants originaires de nombreuses ethnies et tribus de toutes les provinces du Kasaï et du Bandundu[37].

Quatre ans seulement après la fondation de Vaux-sur-Seine, l'École de Théologie Évangélique de Kinshasa (ETEK) est fondée. Elle est issue de la coopération de six dénominations protestantes, dont deux dénominations mennonites, la CMCo et la CEFMC[38]. Depuis, cette école est devenu l'Institut Supérieur de Théologie de Kinshasa pour ensuite faire partie de l'Université chrétienne de Kinshasa (UCKin).

En ce qui concerne le Québec, les Frères mennonites ont mis en place l'In-

---

Goshen Biblical Seminary 1946 ; Mennonite Biblical Seminary 1945 ; Canadian Mennonite Bible College, 1947 ; Eastern Mennonite Seminary, 1948 ; Mennonite Brethren Biblical Seminary 1955 ; AMBS (Elkhart), 1958.

37 *Rythmes anabaptistes*, p. 80 ; Jim Bertsche, *CIM/AIMM : A Story of Vision, Commitment and Grace*, Fairway Press, 1998, p. 100.

38 *Rythmes anabaptistes*, p. 88 ; voir aussi Bertsche, p. 205.

stitut biblique de Laval en 1976, qui est entré en partenariat avec l'Université de Montréal en 1990 et est devenu l'École de Théologie Évangélique de Montréal (ETEM) en 2000. L'ETEM a commencé un partenariat avec l'Institut Biblique Vie de l'Alliance Chrétienne et Missionnaire en 2004, devenant elle aussi inter-dénominationnelle.

Outre le CEFOR/Bienenberg, il n'y a aucune institution mennonite francophone qui offre des cours de théologie de niveau universitaire. Les mennonites francophones, à quelques exceptions près, font de la théologie dans des institutions inter-dénominationnelles évangéliques, comme l'UCKin, la Faculté de Théologie Évangélique de Bangui, la Faculté de Théologie Évangélique des Assemblées Chrétiennes à Abidjan, l'École Supérieure Baptiste de Théologie de l'Afrique de l'Ouest (ESBETAO) à Lomé, la Faculté Libre de Théologie Évangélique de Vaux sur Seine ou l'École de Théologie Évangélique de Montréal.

Formation mennonite ou formation évangélique ?

Les paragraphes précédents font apparaître des trajectoires assez semblables dans des contextes très différents. Ainsi, les histoires mennonites européennes, nord-américaines et africaines sont très liées les unes aux autres. Nous sommes tous marqués d'une manière ou d'une autre par la rencontre entre l'identité mennonite (blessée ou affaiblie) et le monde piétiste ou évangélique. Cette rencontre a engendré un élan missionnaire dans tous les contextes, et expliquent la naissance des églises mennonites au Congo, au Québec ou au Burkina Faso. L'engagement missionnaire des mennonites français au Tchad est aussi à comprendre dans ce contexte[39].

De même, l'entrée dans le monde de la formation théologique « institutionnelle » est un phénomène plutôt récent dans l'histoire mennonite européenne et nord-américaine (la seule exception étant les Pays-Bas). Les Européens et les Nord-Américains ont attendu des siècles, tandis que les Africains y sont arrivés plus rapidement. L'entrée en formation ou la mise en place des institutions de formation a eu lieu à peu près aux mêmes périodes sur les trois continents.

Si les mennonites nord-américains sont assez nombreux pour mettre en place des écoles spécifiquement mennonites, tel n'est pas le cas dans le monde mennonite francophone, que ce soit en Afrique, en Europe ou au Québec. Nous nous formons le plus souvent chez les autres, de même que certains d'entre nous enseignent chez les autres.

---

39 Les mennonites de France ont été présents au Tchad pendant de nombreuses années – et le sont toujours –cependant, l'empreinte évangélique de leur travail a mis l'identité mennonite en arrière-plan.

Ce parcours historique rapide donne lieu à quelques questions et constats avec lesquels nous terminons. D'abord, dans la petite expérience du réseau mennonite francophone, la question de la formation théologique semble être prioritaire. Nous voulons mieux former nos pasteurs et nos prédicateurs pour qu'ils transmettent notre identité théologique mennonite. Cette identité est à vivre et à transmettre au niveau de nos assemblées mais aussi à valoriser auprès des autres.

Le fait qu'il n'existe pas de programme de formation de niveau universitaire spécifiquement mennonite (à part le CEFOR-Bienenberg) est source d'interrogations. Il y a d'abord la question de travailler à l'unité entre chrétiens : le fait d'avoir des facultés communes avec d'autres chrétiens est donc important. L'héritage missionnaire du désir d'unité n'est pas à mépriser. Au contraire, la recherche de la réconciliation et de la paix se trouve au cœur de la théologie anabaptiste. Nous ne pouvons que vouloir travailler avec les autres chrétiens.

Cependant, la capacité de travailler avec d'autres se trouve renforcée lorsqu'on a une identité claire. L'histoire montre que la formation théologique touche de près à l'identité. L'enracinement urbain et libéral du séminaire mennonite d'Amsterdam a contribué à faire disparaître la théologie de la paix. D'autres mennonites européens ont fréquenté les facultés d'État (libérales) ou des instituts bibliques évangéliques. Que l'identité mennonite européenne soit tournée vers le protestantisme libéral ou évangélique, dans les deux cas, la théologie de la paix n'a pas été maintenue. Les mennonites européens ont adopté le nationalisme ambiant issu du siècle des Lumières au point de se trouver dans des armées ennemies. Si les Églises mennonites envoient leurs étudiants « ailleurs », il serait important de trouver des moyens d'enseigner et de maintenir l'identité théologique mennonite. Non pas une identité sectaire ou hostile aux autres, mais plutôt une identité pouvant reconnaître les différences et entrer en dialogue. Cela nécessite des liens et des contacts réguliers et clairs avec les écoles où se forment les mennonites : que ces écoles sachent ce que nous souhaitons et que nous apprenions à collaborer avec elles d'une manière plus consciente.

Comment mettre en place dans chaque contexte des lieux et des moyens pour élaborer et transmettre une identité anabaptiste tout en collaborant avec d'autres ? L'expérience montre qu'une théologie ou missiologie mettant l'accent sur la paix, la justice et la réconciliation peut trouver un écho sérieux chez d'autres chrétiens. Si nous avons à apprendre des autres, nous avons aussi des choses importantes à faire entendre dans le monde chrétien plus large.

Nous manquons de littérature anabaptiste en langue française. Nous commençons petit à petit à combler ce manque, mais il reste des progrès énormes à faire. Comment publier, comment favoriser la publication d'ouvrages de théologie, d'histoire, d'éthique pour l'édification de nos communautés ? Comment mieux partager ce qui est déjà publié ?

Maintenir une identité mennonite, c'est aussi s'intéresser à la mission. Lorsque nous formons des évangélistes et des missionnaires, nous devons intégrer des éléments de missiologie inspirés de la théologie anabaptiste. Trop souvent, du moins en Europe et en Amérique du Nord, ceux qui s'intéressent à la théologie anabaptiste ne s'intéressent pas tellement à la mission et ceux qui s'intéressent à la mission ne voient pas l'intérêt d'intégrer des éléments de théologie anabaptiste dans la missiologie.

C'est grâce aux efforts missionnaires et à la Conférence Mennonite Mondiale qu'il y a aujourd'hui une famille d'Églises mondiales. Cela donne un nouveau contexte pour faire de la théologie et pour « être Église ». Si nous voulons contextualiser correctement nos formations théologiques et nos théologies, nous devons chercher les moyens d'être une famille internationale. L'histoire montre que lorsqu'on reste trop cantonné dans un contexte donné, on peut faire des erreurs énormes. Nous avons besoin les uns des autres. Quelles sont les collaborations souhaitables et possibles ?

Nous avons besoin de prendre au sérieux les possibilités que nous offre la Conférence Mennonite Mondiale, et de favoriser son développement et son rayonnement dans nos contextes respectifs. Elle renforce notre capacité d'être une famille internationale, elle renforce notre identité, elle peut permettre de dépasser les querelles inter-mennonites du passé et d'être en contact et en dialogue avec d'autres chrétiens. Soyons pleinement mennonites, sans orgueil et sans honte. C'est ainsi que nous pouvons le mieux prendre notre place dans la grande famille chrétienne.

A Vision for Global Mission Amidst Shifting Realities

César García[1]

The Anabaptist world has changed since the first global assembly in 1925. One of the changes in the last fourteen years is that Mennonite World Conference (MWC) moved from existing as one event every six years to being a communion of churches. This communion relates in an interdependent way and works on issues of common interest through networks such as the Global Mission Fellowship and Global Anabaptist Service Network, both of which function under the umbrella of the MWC Mission Commission.

This dramatic change has been the result of the missionary movement that has multiplied Anabaptist churches around the world. While the picture of the first global assembly in Switzerland in 1925 shows us only white, Caucasian people, today there are more Anabaptists in Africa, Asia, and Latin America than in countries of the global north. After centuries of following Protestant and evangelical patterns in the sending of missionaries, many churches in the global south have been established and have started to send their own missionaries.

As a result we find ourselves today in a new theological reality shaped by the growth of churches in the global south. Competition among leaders and poor relations between older and younger churches are now the ecclesiastical reality. Our geography has also changed. The classic "fields of mission" are not the same that existed a century ago — we find today missionaries from different cultures around the world going at the same time to the same places. Younger churches have copied northern missiological patterns in their attempt to send missionaries, with the consequence of repeating the same mistakes made by their mother church.

---

1 *César García is General Secretary of Mennonite World Conference.*

A first draft of this article was presented at the Council of International Anabaptist Ministries (CIM) consultation in Chicago on 22 January 2014. The Council consists of seventeen North American-based agencies engaged either directly or indirectly in mission and service abroad. According to its guidelines, the council sponsors "an annual consultation on a topic pertinent to international ministries and church partnerships to facilitate communication and understanding."

The purpose of this writing, after pointing out some of the current realities mentioned before, is to suggest a new missiological paradigm that understands mission, in *addition* to reconciliation, evangelism, and service, as God's activity of bringing together diverse cultures as parts of the same body. In this new paradigm North American agencies can have a leading role in the development of multicultural interdependency, holistic mission, multicultural mission, and the practice of a mission from below.

Let's start by exploring some of the current realities for the global Anabaptist community of around 1.7 million members.

Theological Realities

Pentecostalism is a primary influence and is central to the vibrant worship and spiritual life in the global south. In several Anabaptist churches the pentecostal emphasis on a personal relationship with God, dependency on the Holy Spirit, and the practice of the gifts of the Spirit have been welcomed. However, at the same time, there are often problems among strong leaders, who often don't allow the emergence of new leaders, often resulting in church splits. According to Peter Kuzmic, charisma without character leads to catastrophe.[2] Not all leaders are serving others, and some expect to be served.

Unhealthy conflicts among leaders is one of the reasons why I am concerned about "romantic" views sometimes held in North America that equate global south Pentecostalism with Anabaptism. In Latin America, there are millions of non-Anabaptist Pentecostals, but I am not aware of any who are pacifists. Some varieties of Pentecostalism are identified with consumerism and the prosperity gospel, rather than being known for speaking the message of the kingdom of Christ, justice for society, peacemaking, and Christ crucified. René Padilla argues that these churches have adopted the "mass empire" culture, as they use business strategies and marketing techniques to reach their numerical goals, offering material prosperity, making people feel good, and emphasizing entertainment.[3] Pentecostalism does not automatically mean Anabaptism.

On the other hand, we must not reject the many healthy values that Pentecostalism brings to us. Vibrant worship and a life of personal devotion, an emphasis on evangelism and priesthood of all believers through the development

---

2 Peter Kuzmic cited by Samuel Escobar, "The Global Scenario at the Turn of the Century," in *Global Missiology for the 21st Century: The Iguassu Dialogue*, ed. William David Taylor (Grand Rapids, MI: Baker Academic, 2000), 38.

3 René Padilla cited by Milton Acosta, "Power Pentecostalisms: The 'Non-Catholic' Latin American Church is Going Full Steam Ahead — But Are We on the Right Track?" *Christianity Today* (July 29, 2009).

of gifts — and practice of all gifts (including healing, prophecy, and speaking in tongues), among other values, have been crucial for Christians in Latin America. People that face injustice and suffering find in them the strength and inspiration that they need to overcome those situations.

We need to avoid both "Charismania" and "Charisphobia." We need both Anabaptist and pentecostal values and commitment. I urge North American agencies: in your ministry, don't forget the Anabaptist values such as community, peacemaking, evangelism, leadership understood as service, and the important role of the Holy Spirit in the life of the church. Anabaptist values are not cultural attachments to the gospel. They are a very important part of the core of the gospel, thus a real need around the world.

Ecclesiastical Realities

Emerging churches have had relationships with agencies rather than church to church. According to Pakisa Tshimika and Tim Lind,

> Many churches have strong historic connections to the churches that were instrumental in initiating and/or nurturing them. But these relationships have almost always been between a church and an agency rather than between the two churches directly. As a result, initiating churches often find themselves with no direct relationship to churches they have supported for many years, and younger churches find themselves linked not to a church but to a specialized agency, which historically mediates relationships with other parts of the denominational family.[4]

This reality began to change in the last twenty-five years. Examples of this progressive change have been the creation of ICOMB (International Community of Mennonite Brethren) and IBICA (International Brethren in Christ Association). These two entities are an attempt to link churches inside of their own constituency. There have also been efforts to develop mission-to-mission relations inside of the Mennonite church and of the Mennonite Brethren Church. However, some of these church plants feel alone for a variety of reasons. Due to the financial reality that they face, the withdrawal of the support that was received from their mother church for many years has left them with the feeling of being abandoned. Additionally, in many of the global south cultures, when suffering or conflict occurs, relationships and global connections are the only tools that they have to overcome difficult circumstances. If a church finds itself without global relationships, the strength and hope that they need to face those

---

4 Pakisa K. Tshimika, Tim Lind, and Mennonite World Conference, *Sharing Gifts in the Global Family of Faith: One Church's Experiment* (Intercourse, PA: Good, 2003), 99.

circumstances are missed.

The need of interdependency, global relationships, and mutual support may be some of the reasons why MWC has changed during this time from an every six-year event to a "communion" or movement that facilitates connections of churches in order to work on issues of common interest. I think about MWC as an organic movement that supports church-to-church relationships in a global way, in South-to-South relationships as well, rather than always only North-to-South.

Geographical Realities

Looking at the global membership of Mennonite and Brethren in Christ churches we can see that the large churches are in the global south, with very little presence in the Middle East and North Africa regions. This means that even though several of the Anabaptist agencies are working in the Middle East and North Africa, MWC is lacking the perspective of followers of Christ from these areas. MWC needs the presence of Christians from the Middle East and North Africa. In these places there are many churches that do not have the name "Mennonite." However, this should not be an obstacle for having them enrich our global communion. We want to be — and need to be — a movement of Anabaptists from the entire world.

Another geographical reality is that the idea of mission is growing in the global south, but the global south does not have the same resources that the global north has. This may be a reason why "a focus on global mission reflects older churches, while a focus on local mission characterizes younger churches," according to Conrad Kanagy, Tilahun Beyene, and Richard Showalter.[5]

Many of the same mistakes made by our North American agencies that have received criticism are now made by global south agencies: imposing foreign cultures, lack of Anabaptist values, or identity, paternalism, and lack of personal care. William Taylor explains: "We are all familiar with the historic three 'selfs' of the church: self-supporting, self-propagating, self-governing. But today's reality is more complex, richer, and more challenging, for there are really five 'selfs.' These include the known three, plus self-theologizing and self-missiologizing."[6] Working and walking with younger churches and their mission agencies are crucial parts of the challenge facing North American agencies. Younger churches need to develop contextualized Anabaptist theol-

---

5 Conrad L. Kanagy, Tilahun Beyene, and Richard Showalter, *Winds of the Spirit: A Profile of Anabaptist Churches in the Global South* (Harrisonburg, VA: Herald, 2012), 169.

6 Taylor, *Global Missiology for the 21st Century*, 6.

ogy and missional principles that are not just a translation of foreign writings but a genuine result of a serious interaction and reflection on the realities of the context in which they live. Although this may be happening in some contexts it is not yet a generalized experience in the global south. The method and process of reaching theological and missiological contextualization can be learned from older churches and agencies from the global north. To learn about the experience of others by serving alongside them will facilitate this process.

Missiological Realities

The way of Jesus needs to be central to the missional task. I encourage leaders and churches to question cultural patterns that don't affirm servant leadership, mutual accountability, or other Anabaptist faith practices that are crucial to a vibrant faith community. And I challenge the mission agencies to communicate, collaborate, and work together for the growth of the church. Taylor mentions the following over-simplifications that have been made in the international evangelical missionary movement:

- The crippling omissions in the Great Commission — reducing it to proclamation alone — which lead to only a partial understanding of the mission of the church, resulting in spiritual anemia and a thin veneer of Christianity, regardless of culture or nation.
- The absence of a robust gospel of the kingdom which calls us to radical commitment and discipleship to Christ.
- An inadequate theology of suffering and martyrdom . . . .
- An over-emphasis on short-term missions that minimizes longer-term service, and an inadequate biblical theology of vocation.
- The illusion by some that mass media is the final answer to world evangelization or the suggestion that "the church finally has the technology to finish the Great Commission," whether the Internet, mass communication, publication, or other media. The danger is obvious, for it disregards the sacrificial, incarnational calling of God into our world of profound personal, familial, socio-economic, cultural, and environmental crises.[7]

A New Missiological Paradigm

Anabaptist agencies need a new paradigm for mission. The goal is not simply to flip the power relationships between the agents and assumed recipients of

---

7 Ibid., 4–5.

mission, but rather to change the basic assumption of mission altogether — to align with God's mission of bringing together the diverse cultures from around the world. The call, which Emmanuel Katongole names as the "Ephesian Moment," is to understand mission, in *addition* to reconciliation, evangelism, and service, as God's activity of bringing together diverse social fragments — as parts of the same body — so as to realize what Paul describes as the "very height of Christ's full stature."[8]

According to Ephesians, the "aha" moment of reaching the full stature of Christ happens when we are sitting at the same table, eating with people from different cultures. In this multicultural environment we see the complete image of Jesus. No single culture sees the complete image. When part of the body is not present, the picture is incomplete. In the same way, the book of Revelation is calling us to live right now according to that vision. We need a new paradigm, which involves sitting together, and finding the meaning of Christ's witness.

Given the need of a new paradigm that involves the "Ephesian Moment," what might be the role of our North American agencies in a paradigm that involves a multicultural and interdependent witness? I offer the following suggestions about the future place of North American mission agencies:

A leading role in interdependency

Agencies must speak with each other or the witness is negatively impacted. Some Colombians were surprised that there is something called "Council of International Ministries (CIM)" and that different agencies of different Anabaptist churches (and of mission and service!) are actually meeting together. There are differences, but we love each other and need to talk with each other. Let us be guided by a vision of Anabaptist agencies working together in church planting, peacemaking, health, education, and service. Multicultural and holistic teams working together are a powerful witness. In places where there are separated ministries or agencies, let's bring those teams together at least to pray and tell the story, making it visible in a global way.

A leading role in holistic mission

The implicitly received message in the South in the past has been that service and mission agencies can't work together. However, in many places in the global south, churches practice holistic ministry without distinction between word,

---

8 Emmanuel Katongole, "Mission and the Ephesian Moment of World Christianity: Pilgrimages of Pain and Hope and the Economics of Eating Together," *Mission Studies*, 29 (2012): 183–200.

deed, and being.[9]

MWC is structured now to facilitate interdependency, multicultural witness, and experiential learning through our networks of agencies — the Global Mission Fellowship and the Global Anabaptist Service Network. We need to avoid the specialization and fragmentation that is typical of modernity and move to practical and relational experiences of holistic ministries that honor specialization without falling into separation.

A leading role in multicultural mission

Some agencies that are hesitant to work with multicultural teams in practice do not celebrate cultural differences, but only tolerate them. I propose testing the "cooperative model" mentioned by Samuel Escobar:

> In the cooperative model, churches from rich nations add their material resources to the human resources of the churches in poor nations in order to work in a third area … but the model poses some practical questions for which there are no easy answers, one of them being the raising of support for non-Western participants. The traditional Catholic missionary orders such as Franciscans or Jesuits, which are supranational, provide the oldest and more developed example, facilitated by the vows of poverty, celibacy, and obedience.[10]

What would happen if we looked at the missional monastic roots of Anabaptism? Franciscans influenced the Anabaptist movement in its beginnings. This monastic, missionary Catholic order practiced a multicultural communal way of sending missionaries based on a vow of poverty. Could we learn from Catholic orders about how to structure a multicultural team that bears witness to Christ? Anabaptist agencies have followed Protestant patterns of missions for many years. Could this be a time to turn to monastic patterns to learn from them on issues such as administration, multicultural teams, holistic ministries, and mission from below?

A leading place on the mission from below

Some persons from the South think that if they go into mission, then their lifestyle will be similar to North American missionaries or service workers. According to Taylor,

> Before any "practical" training for mission in the use of methods and tools for the verbal communication of a message, it is imperative to form disciples for *a new style of missionary presence*. Mission requires orthopraxis as

---

9 Kanagy, Beyene, and Showalter, *Winds of the Spirit*, 170.
10 Escobar, "Global Scenario," 34.

well as orthodoxy . . . . This Christological model that was also the pattern under which Paul and the other apostles placed their own missionary practice could be described as "mission from below."[11]

What would happen if, following the example of monastic orders, there would be a "vow of poverty" in multicultural teams for everyone? A mission that would invite members to renounce comfort? What would happen if there were more teams — as they are in some agencies — that are called to simple lifestyle and holistic ministry, while respecting and honoring specialization such as church planting, conflict resolution, and service? Some attempts at a cooperative model between North American agencies and South agencies have failed because of huge financial disparities among members of the same team. An Anabaptist emphasis on simplicity as a requirement for each member of the team, regardless of the country of origin, might help us solve many problems.

In conclusion, let me highlight some principles for God's mission taken from the document "Christian Witness in a Multi-Religious World" Recommendations for Conduct, developed by the World Council of Churches, the Pontifical Council for Interreligious Dialogue, and the World Evangelical Alliance:

- Acting in God's love.
- Imitating Jesus Christ.
- Christian virtues. Christians are called to conduct themselves with integrity, charity, compassion, and humility, and to overcome all arrogance, condescension and disparagement (cf. Galatians 5:22).
- Acts of service and justice. Acts of service, such as providing education, health care, relief services and acts of justice and advocacy are an integral part of witnessing to the gospel.
- Discernment in ministries of healing. As an integral part of their witness to the gospel, Christians exercise ministries of healing.
- Rejection of violence.

---

11 Ibid., 43.

I finish here with the words of Juan Martínez and Mark Branson: "We can shape intercultural community in [agencies] not by ignoring particulars but by affirming our accountability and shared missional life."[12]

May God lead us in this purpose!

---

12 Mark Lau Branson and Juan Francisco Martínez, *Churches, Cultures, and Leadership: A Practical Theology of Congregations and Ethnicities* (Downers Grove, IL: IVP Academic, 2011), Chapter 3.

Striving Towards Dependence:

An Alternative Mennonite Anthropological Witness in Late Modernity

JASON GREIG[1]

Abstract:
Few things appear as self-evident and unquestionable for the moral life in Western late modernity than the absolute good of independence and autonomy. The identity of this "reflexive self" consists of being choosers and consumers, self-producing life from the unlimited options presented by Western liberalism. Recent Mennonite theologizing around the practices of baptism and foot washing shows an affinity for this independent self, and thus potentially shares in its vulnerability to the destructive aspects of consumer capitalism. This article posits that a more authentic Christian identity lies in being a dependent creature, who receives its self from God and the church rather than from its own self-production. By recognizing her need for God and the church, the Christian eludes the domain of consumer capitalism and offers a bold alternative witness to the world. This article will offer suggestions on how the Mennonite practices of baptism and foot washing might be recovered and reimagined to form Christian disciples more faithfully into followers of Jesus.

In him we live and move and have our being (Acts 17:28).

To be Christian means that we must be embedded in practices so materially constitutive of our communities that we are not tempted to describe our lives in the language offered by the world, that is, the language of choice. Only then will Christians be able to challenge an all too tolerant world that celebrates many gods as alternatives to the One God who alone is worthy of worship.[2]

---

1 *Jason Reimer Greig is an MDiv graduate of Anabaptist Mennonite Biblical Seminary and is currently pursuing further doctoral studies.*

This article was prepared for the "Wading Deeper: Anabaptist-Mennonite Identities Engage Postmodernity" conference which took place May 30–June 1, 2014 at Canadian Mennonite University in Winnipeg, Manitoba, Canada. I wish to thank the Toronto Mennonite Theological Centre, which organized the event, particularly John Rempel for his insight and support.

2 Stanley Hauerwas, *Wilderness Wanderings: Probing Twentieth-Century Theology and Philosophy* (Boulder, CO: Westview, 1997), 116–7.

Few things appear as self-evident and unquestionable for the moral life in Western late modernity than the absolute good of independence and autonomy. Whether in regards to raising children, empowering marginalized persons to participate in social life, or encouraging people to make their own health care decisions, an impulse of liberal society rests in individuals pursuing independence as a requisite to human flourishing. In this context, human identity consists of being *choosers* and *consumers*, self-producing life from the unlimited options presented by Western liberalism.

But does this vision of the individual as self-originating maker accurately denote human identity? And if not, does the church offer a compelling alternative to this view? As Mennonite Christians living in Western, late modern society,[3] it is tempting to understand the church as being composed merely of voluntaristic, consensual individuals who freely choose to gather and share life together. Yet this view alone misses crucial dimensions of human life and risks turning Christians into isolated monads autonomously producing their own faith. An identity as independent chooser not only fails to speak truthfully to the human condition, but also entraps persons in the forces of consumer capitalism and marginalizes those vulnerable persons whose ability for purposive agency remains highly limited.[4]

This article will argue that the autonomous self of late modernity misrepresents human identity, and excessively advocates independence as a nonnegotiable human good. Relying so heavily on independence not only alienates persons from one another, but also places persons firmly within the domain of consumer capitalism. A brief look at contemporary popular theologizing re-

---

3 This article will intentionally refer to the contemporary period in the west as being that of "late modernity" rather than the more common "postmodernity." While the "post" of postmodernity can mean the situation following in the wake of modernity, the popular use of the term often means instead the supposed closure of modernity and the birth of a new age. I understand this view as being somewhat premature and potentially missing the continuities of the present time with that of the modern period. See Anthony Giddens, *The Consequences of Modernity* (Stanford, CA: Stanford University Press, 1991), and Zygmunt Bauman, *Liquid Modernity* (Cambridge: Polity, 2000).

4 Consumer capitalism — sometimes referred to as "late capitalism" — differs from "free-market" capitalism by its need to manufacture needs rather than goods in order to maintain growth and production. In a world already saturated with basic goods, corporations require the consumption of ever higher levels of superfluous products to sustain growth targets. For more, see Anastasios S. Korkotsides, *Consumer Capitalism* (London: Routledge, 2007), and Benjamin Barber, *Consumed: How Markets Corrupt Children, Infantilize Adults, and Swallow Citizens Whole* (New York: W. W. Norton, 2007), esp. chap. 2.

veals that North American Mennonites are highly susceptible to unconsciously accepting this mythic self. Recovering and returning to a human identity as dependent creatures potentially offers a more authentic vision of human flourishing, while also presenting an emboldened witness to the excesses of late modern liberalism.

After articulating some methodological assumptions and limitations, this article will begin by articulating the terrain of late modern identity. The social imaginary and practices of the late modern character reveal a highly "reflexive self," which conceives of itself as maker of its own destiny and embodies this view through discursive and bodily practices. This project will then show how recent reflections from Mennonites on the ecclesial practices of baptism and foot washing potentially cohere too closely with late modernity's reflexive self. Following this will be a consideration of Christian identity as being a dependent creature, recognizing the inherent need of humans for God, others, and the world. Finally, suggestions will be given on how the Mennonite practices of baptism and foot washing might be reimagined to enable them to form Christians more accurately into authentic followers of Jesus.

Starting Points: Methodological Assumptions and Limitations

A feature of late modernity is the demand to state one's positions and assumptions clearly before proceeding with one's argument. This article will respect this principle by stating some methodological assumptions and limitations of this work.

Independence as a relative good

The critique of the independent, reflexive self of late modernity offered here does not include a claim that autonomy and agency represent evils or absolute distortions of being human. The capacities of independence and autonomy can assist in furthering human flourishing, and thus represent human goods. Yet this article will insist on autonomy as a relative good, rather than the absolute good often advocated for in late modernity. In other words, independence always remains dependent on other religious and social factors in claiming to be a human good. The goal of autonomy does not require elimination, but must always be sought in terms of "relational autonomy,"[5] "dependent agency,"[6] or

---

5 See the collection of essays in Catriona Mackenzie and Natalie Stoljar, eds., *Relational Autonomy: Feminist Perspectives on Autonomy, Agency, and the Social Self* (Oxford: Oxford University Press, 2000).

6 Leslie Pickering Francis and Anita Silvers, "Liberalism and Individually Scripted Ideas of the Good: Meeting the Challenge of Dependent Agency," *Social Theory and Practice* 33, no. 2 (April 2007): 311–34.

"dependent-independence."[7]

This article will follow feminist moral philosopher Eva Feder Kittay's suggestion that morality and anthropology must begin not with the autonomy of the isolated individual, but with the inherent vulnerability and dependence of human life. Kittay boldly wishes to relativize the contemporary use of "interdependence" in describing the human good. For Kittay, too often interdependence means "simply the mutual (often voluntary) cooperation between essentially independent persons."[8] In privileging dependency, Kittay wishes not to deny human interdependence but to "find a knife sharp enough to cut through the fiction of our independence."[9] Such an intense focus on independence not only speaks untruthfully to the human condition, but also threatens to place particularly vulnerable persons in a subhuman status. At the same time, this article will assume that this illusion of the autonomous self acts as a pernicious myth for *all* human persons.

An article grounded in the community of L'Arche

This article could not have been conceived or written without the author's eleven years of participation in two Canadian L'Arche communities. This international federation of communities of people with and without intellectual disabilities sharing faith and life together represents not just good service provision. Rather, they act as alternative moral communities which expand the ethical imagination. Living and becoming friends with people with cognitive impairments challenged my own unconscious belief in the autonomous individual and forced me to acknowledge the inherently relational dimension of human beings. I discovered quickly in my graduate studies that respecting the lives of those I had lived with would compel me to take dependency seriously.

The culture of L'Arche conceives of the dependency of people with cognitive impairments not as "problems" to be ameliorated, but as a constitutive aspect of being human. Kittay's fear of the dominant myth of the independent self casting long shadows on those with cognitive impairments becomes very evident when sharing life with these persons. The grace of communities like L'Arche rests in their exposing of this illusion, and converting the nondisabled to acknowledge dependence as a potential means to relationship rather than an

7 John Swinton, Harriet Mowat, and Susannah Baines, "Whose Story Am I? Profound Intellectual Disability in the Kingdom of God," *Journal of Religion, Disability & Health* 15, no. 1 (Jan–March 2011): 5–19.

8 Eva Feder Kittay, *Love's Labor: Essays on Women, Equality, and Dependency* (New York: Routledge, 1999), xii.

9 Kittay, *Love's Labor*, xiii.

absolute impediment to independence.

The benefits and limitations of context

The context of this article rests in Mennonite identity within a Western, liberal, specifically North American society, which also stands as the social position of the author. It is incumbent to acknowledge that this represents a limitation in regards to speaking about Mennonite identity in late modernity. The self-evident fact that most Mennonites reside outside of North America and Western Europe means that the analysis and conclusions of this article remain partial for the global Mennonite community. Insights and reflections of Mennonites in the two-thirds world, where the autonomous self has less of a hold on the moral imagination, must be sought because they will only enrich the contemporary discussion on identity. These voices are crucial in presenting a different conception of identity and human being to those of us in the enculturated West, and challenging our capitulations to the myth of the independent individual.[10] At the same time, reflections on being Mennonite in the one-third world can offer evidence for the fruitful discernment for Mennonites in the global South of the benefits and limitations of Western late modernity. Thus even despite its weaknesses, hopefully this project will find points of connection with others in the global Mennonite/Anabaptist family.

On being a Mennonite (in late modernity)

Keeping in mind the unstable and tenuous concept of identity, this article assumes the notion of a discernable Mennonite identity. While no longer requiring a North European ethnicity, the following discussion supposes that being a Mennonite in late modernity rests in being historically and theologically connected with the sixteenth-century Anabaptist reformers. This article assumes that being Mennonite also acknowledges the debt contemporary Mennonites have to the diverse array of congregations which attempted to live out the Anabaptist story in the centuries which followed the Radical Reformation. Thus Mennonite identity is not merely ethical or social or confessional but also *ecclesial*; being a Mennonite requires not just belief or just ethics, but also demands being part of a body of believers who discern the workings of the Holy Spirit in the congregation and the world.

While this article does not wish to repeat John D. Thiesen's wish to "bury"

---

10 For example, the African-initiated theology of Ubuntu offers a radically different theological anthropology, much more ready to accept the inherently social and dependent nature of human life. For a Christian articulation of Ubuntu, see Michael Battle, *Ubuntu: I in You and You in Me* (New York: Seabury, 2009), and *Reconciliation: The Ubuntu Theology of Desmond Tutu* (Cleveland, OH: Pilgrim, 1997).

the recent trend to remake all things Mennonite into "Anabaptist," I do share his warning about the temptation to jettison (the often messy) four centuries of Mennonite history in favor of a supposed pristine Anabaptist foundation.[11] Thus this article leans heavily on the language of "Mennonite" rather than "Anabaptist" in describing the thought and practice which undergird contemporary views of Mennonite identity. This is not meant to disqualify those congregations practicing faith under the banner of (Neo-) Anabaptism, but only point to a desire to root this examination in a historical and living instantiation of faith called "Mennonite." Hopefully those calling themselves Anabaptists can benefit from any of the insights which result and linger from the following discussion.

The Reflexive Self of Late Modernity

One cannot begin to sketch the terrain of the late modern self without also mentioning the birth of modernity which arose out of the Enlightenment. Ideas such as the turn to the subject, individual freedom, and human progress cannot be understood without placing them within the context of the paradigm shift that occurred in Western Europe after the Reformation. Enlightenment thinkers believed that this new era represented a chance for humans to transcend the limitations of contingency through a greater control over the natural world. And along with the mastery of the environment came more mastery over one's own life situation.

With the emergence of modernity came the notion that the good life includes the intentional choosing of one's identity and conception of the good, what philosopher Charles Taylor refers to as "authenticity."[12] Conceptions of identity in antiquity through to the Middle Ages placed the person firmly within their social context, and determined to a large degree people's vocations and identities. Identities were as much received as created in this milieu, and thus remained mostly fixed by kinship relations and larger social factors. Along with the Enlightenment's turn to the subject came the desire to free the self from the tyrannical external imposition of identity, and place it in the hands of the individual. Authenticity and autonomous subjectivity increasingly became incorporated into conceptions of the good life. Impediments to an authentic choosing of one's good came to be seen either as, at its most benign, obstacles

---

11 John D. Thiesen, "To Bury, Not to Praise," in *Anabaptist Vision for the New Millenium*, eds. Dale Schrag and James Juhnke (Kitchener, Ont.: Pandora, 2000), 124.

12 For Taylor's articulation and history of the rise of authenticity as a marker of Western identity, see his *The Ethics of Authenticity* (Cambridge, MA: Harvard University Press, 1992), and *A Secular Age* (Cambridge, MA: Harvard University Press, 2007).

to be transcended or, at worst, oppressive social imaginaries to be conquered and eliminated.

One can see this view of morality in the work of the influential political theorist John Rawls. Rawls takes as axiomatic that persons in liberal societies possess the autonomous subjectivity and independence to conceive their own good.[13] People require these capacities because of the lack of consensus on moral notions of justice, and thus each must decide for her- or himself their own *telos*. However, this demand is not due merely to a lack of societal notions of the common good, but rather meets the need for an "authentic" and happy life. Thus for Rawls, "the good is what is *for him* the most rational long-term plan of life given reasonably favorable circumstances. A man is happy when he is more or less successfully in the way of carrying out this plan. To put it briefly, the good is the satisfaction of rational desire."[14] According to Rawls, the good must be centered in the individual, and must be self-originating and independent, freed from external impositions of the good from other individuals and institutions. Once persons arrive at their own notions of the good, they can then negotiate and intentionally enter into contractual relations with others also pursuing their own life plans.

Unbounded from external forces imposing kinship or social identities, the self becomes free to create and pursue its own notions of the good. This results in what sociologist Anthony Giddens refers to as the "reflexive self" of late modernity. According to Giddens, no longer does the self merely have a choice as to its self-identity, but now it must constantly choose and discern its own story amidst a plethora of competing options.

> In the post-traditional order of modernity . . . self-identity becomes a re-flexively organized endeavour. The reflexive project of the self, which consists in the sustaining of coherent, yet continuously revised, biographical narratives, takes place in the context of multiple choice as filtered through abstract systems. In modern social life, the notion of lifestyle takes on a particular significance. The more tradition loses its hold, and the more daily life is reconstituted in terms of the dialectical interplay of the local and the global, the more individuals are forced to negotiate lifestyle choices among a diversity of options.[15]

---

13 John Rawls, "Justice as Fairness: Political not Metaphysical," *Philosophy and Public Affairs* 14, no. 3 (1985): 240.

14 John Rawls, *A Theory of Justice* (Cambridge, MA: Harvard University Press, 1971), 92–3.

15 Anthony Giddens, *Modernity and Self-identity: Self and Society in the Late Modern Age* (Stanford, CA: Stanford University Press, 1991), 5.

For the authentic person of late modernity, the good life demands the "reflexive awareness" which constantly monitors the circumstances of life to make sure they match their own chosen "lifestyle." Entailed in this awareness is the notion that self-identity "is not something just given . . . but something that has to be routinely created and sustained in the reflexive activities of the individual."[16]

When identity becomes a matter of continual (re-)creation rather than open reception, *choice* becomes an absolute requirement for a healthy sense of self. According to theologian Hans Reinders, personal choice as a means for self-expression and self-affirmation dominates the narrative of contemporary society. This "choosing self":

> presupposes that the good life for human beings is coextensive with a chosen life. What follows is that "goodness" and "meaning" is conferred on people's lives by virtue of their own authorization . . . . [T]his is usually expressed by the claim that people need to be respected as "the authors" of their own lives . . . . In order to have a life that is properly called "good," they must be in control of how they choose to live their lives.[17]

The choosing self can only conceive of the good in regards to a life self-imagined and self-created. Those features of life which appear as "givens," as persistent aspects of identity which contradict or impede individual life plans, come to be seen as objects of suspicion eligible for elimination or modification. In this view, all things exist merely as malleable tools for individual self-expression.

At the same time, valorizing choice to such a degree sits well with consumer capitalism. The fundamental orientation of the late modern self is as *consumer* and *chooser* of a myriad of "lifestyles" and self-made identities. In a culture of planned obsolescence and 24/7 shopping, the need for constant monitoring and tweaking of identity demanded by the reflexive self finds a ready partner in the malls and box stores of most North American urban centers. If late modernity has expressed a pervasive distrust of meta-narratives, the human story which capitalism embodies and promotes has more than weathered the storm and escaped close scrutiny.

A quick glance at the late modern bodily practice of cosmetic surgery reveals this reflexive self in action. Formerly the practice of the "rich and famous," cosmetic surgery has increasingly become accessible to the point of sometimes

---

16 Giddens, *Modernity and Self-identity*, 52.

17 Hans S. Reinders, *Receiving the Gift of Friendship: Profound Disability, Theological Anthropology, and Ethics* (Grand Rapids, MI: Eerdmans, 2008), 136.

becoming merely a "medical" procedure.[18] The "reflexive project" of the late modern self consists not only in creating abstract conceptions of the good. In addition, the reflexive self manipulates and modifies the body as a tool for carrying out its life plan and a means of expressing its created identity. As feminist Kathy Davis explains:

> Cosmetic surgery is not about beauty, but about identity. For a woman who feels trapped in a body which does not fit her sense of who she is, cosmetic surgery becomes a way to renegotiate identity through her body . . . . For a woman whose suffering has gone beyond a certain point, cosmetic surgery can become a matter of justice — the only fair thing to do.[19]

When the body does not match the identity of the autonomous choosing self, it must be shaped to match the individual's self-originating conception of the good life/body.

In this "makeover culture," the individual transformation of the self is not just encouraged but *demanded*.[20] Carl Elliot sees this attitude alive and well in the rise of the use of enhancement procedures in the USA. In an era where people conceive of themselves as managers of life projects, self-fulfillment becomes not a gift to be received in community but a demand and duty to be made and created.

> Once self-fulfillment is hitched to the success of a human life, it comes perilously close to an obligation – not an obligation to God, country, or family, but an obligation to the self. We are compelled to pursue fulfillment

---

18 For numbers in the USA, see the website for The American Society for Aesthetic Plastic Surgery, "Cosmetic Surgery Increase in 2012," accessed May 15, 2013. http://www.surgery.org/media/news-releases/cosmetic-procedures-increase-in-2012. Lest one think cosmetic procedures merely a phenomenon in overdeveloped countries, see the figures from the website for the International Society of Aesthetic Plastic Surgery (ISAPS). "ISAPS International Survey on Aesthetic/Cosmetic Procedures Performed in 2011," accessed May 10, 2013. http://www.isaps.org/isaps-global-statistics-2012.html. For numbers for Canada, see the ISAPS report.

19 Kathy Davis, *Reshaping the Female Body: The Dilemma of Cosmetic Surgery* (New York: Routledge, 1995), 163.

20 Meredith Jones explains "makeover culture" as when "Self-renovation by whatever means is compulsory and never-ending. Self-improvement is something that makeover culture insists everyone needs: it is a continuing enterprise that may be realised via home renovation, lifelong learning, career enhancement or body-work such as cosmetic surgery. Good citizens in makeover culture are in a permanent state of becoming something better." *Skintight: An Anatomy of Cosmetic Surgery* (Oxford: Berg, 2008), 57.

through enhancement technologies not in order to get ahead of others, but to make sure that we have lived our lives to the fullest.[21]

And rather than freeing the self, Elliot sees the drive for self-determination as firmly placing people within the domain of consumer capitalism.

One also sees the choosing self alive and well in the Western discursive practice of advertising. In previous eras, marketers directed consumers to external exemplars and models of perfection through "aspirational" marketing. However, Steve Maich and Lianne George claim that now goods are sold through the constant affirmation of the individual as the center of the universe. Maich and George call this the "You Sell." "Where marketers used to primarily sell products or brand values, they're now selling You — an idealized, self-actualized version of yourself — back to you . . . . *You* are the real good. We — or rather You — have become the only real product anyone is pushing."[22] As identity becomes more and more a self-originating product, corporations are more than happy to assist individuals in building their patchwork selves. Thus Dell offers, for example, customized computers not as appliances but as extensions of self-identity. While the illusion of consumer control is maintained, Maich and George claim that the You Sell only cements the power of marketers in defining the late modern self as a "super-consumer."[23]

Thus while the reflexive self of late modernity aspires to independence in order to make its own life and good, it still remains firmly within the grip of external forces of control. As it constantly maintains its self-originating identity, the choosing self distances itself from others and looks with suspicion on the givenness of life. Anything outside the control of the late modern self can only be conceived as an impediment to its life plan and thus in need of elimination or modification. Yet the choosing self remains highly vulnerable to the manipulations of corporations, continually selling brands as customizations of individual identity.

---

21 Carl Elliot, *Better Than Well: American Medicine Meets the American Dream* (New York: W. W. Norton, 2003), 303.

22 Steve Maich and Lianne George, *The Ego Boom: Why the World Really Revolves Around You* (Toronto: Key Porter, 2009), 20.

23 "Out of the triumph of the You Sell has evolved a breed of super-consumers, whose spending habits are driven by the desire to express themselves. In this world, consumption becomes a kind of performance, limited . . . by the availability of credit." Maich and George, *The Ego Boom*, 70.

Mennonite Theology and Praxis Meet the Reflexive Self

How do contemporary Mennonites fare in regards to the dominance of the re-flexive self of late modernity? Certainly one could argue that communal bonds in Mennonite communities have weathered the storm of North American hy-per-individualism. Yet the highly subjectivist and agential bias of Western faith leaves Mennonite identity susceptible to some of the excesses of the reflexive self, particularly when notions of identity are assimilated unintentionally from the broader culture.

A first glance at early sixteenth-century Anabaptist thought reveals a po-tentially ambivalent legacy. One can certainly pick up signs of the need for a highly subjective and intentional choosing self. The Radical Reformers clearly believed that faith must originate in the individual, not in external institutions or social pressures. Being identified as a Christian or becoming a member of the church required a previous *decision*, encountered and arrived at within the subjective individual. Authentic Christian faith must begin from within the individual through an intentional and rational choice to follow Christ.

Yet one should exercise caution before too quickly attributing ideas of a late modern reflexive self onto the sixteenth-century Radical Reformers. It is a continual temptation to project notions of autonomous agency onto people in antiquity and the Middle Ages.[24] According to the late Mennonite theologian James Reimer, free will for medieval persons always emanated first from God's prevenient calling. "In the premodern voluntarist tradition, free will was ulti-mately derivative, and subordinate to the mystery of divine will, election, and providence."[25] The demand to continuously monitor and autonomously choose for one's self was a foreign concept for medieval Europeans, the Radical Re-formers included. Faith for these latter persons was never a matter of mere reflexive decision, but always depended on the work and action of God and the Holy Spirit.

Late modern Mennonites, however, do not have the same culture with which to formulate identity. Mennonite theologians have expressed concern at the high levels of subjectivism and individualism present in some Mennonite

---

24 See Timothy Reiss, *Mirages of the Selfe: Patterns of Personhood in Ancient and Early Modern Europe* (Stanford: Stanford University Press, 2003).

25 A. James Reimer, "Christian Anthropology: The Perils of the Believers Church View of the *Humanum*," in *Mennonites and Classical Theology* (Kitchener, Ont.: Pandora, 2001), 536.

practice.[26] Whether this reflexivity comes through North American revivalism's emphasis on personal conversion, or in more liberal stresses on activism, Mennonite faith communities risk becoming mere voluntaristic associations of like-minded, Rawlsian individuals. As Reimer mentions, "with the radical nominalism of the modern period, and the loss of all sense of transcendent realism, voluntarism as understood by the Believers Church is in danger of undermining the very ethic it once sought to undergird."[27] The independent choosers advocated in some current reflections of Mennonite practice come to look dangerously similar to that of late modernity's reflexive self. A brief look at contemporary practice of the ordinances of baptism and foot washing will illustrate how the choosing self reveals itself in the Mennonite ordinances of baptism and foot washing.

In *Ask Third Way Café*, Jodi Nisly Hertzler relates answers to queries made on the *Third Way Café* website by people expressing interest in Mennonite faith and practice. In response to the question "What is accomplished by waiting to baptize members?" Hertzler gives the following answer:

> the benefit is that only people who have deliberately made the choice to be baptized are in fact baptized. The choice to live a Christ-centered life is not an easy one. It's a major commitment that a person makes to God and to the church family, and it's not to be taken lightly. When an infant is baptized, the sacrament seems to Mennonites to lose some power, as it reflects the parents' beliefs and not the child's . . . . [W]e reserve baptism for people who can make the choice for themselves and can understand the meaning of what they are doing . . . . We believe the church is strengthened when made up of adults who have made the decision to follow Christ and be baptized and can remember the impact of that ceremony in their Christian walk.[28]

The emphasis on choice and decision in this response could not be clearer. In this conception, faith is for those who can intentionally choose from various options, and originates in the individual rather than external forces (like

---

26 For examples, see Marlin E. Miller, "The Mennonites," in *Baptism & Church: A Believers' Church Vision*, ed. Merle D. Strege (Grand Rapids, MI: Sagamore, 1986), 23–24, and "Baptism in the Mennonite Tradition," in *Baptism, Peace, and the State in the Reformed and Mennonite Traditions*, eds. Ross T. Bender and Alan P. F. Sell (Waterloo, Ont.: Wilfrid Laurier University Press for the Calgary Institute for the Humanities, 1991), 53–54. See also John D. Roth, *Practices: Mennonite Worship and Witness* (Scottdale, PA: Herald, 2009), 199–200.

27 Reimer, "Christian Anthropology," 536.

28 Jodi Nisly Hertzler, *Ask Third Way Café: 50 Common and Quirky Questions about Mennonites* (Telford, PA: Cascadia, 2009), 22–23.

parents). The demand for memory implied in this statement coheres with the reflexive self's need to monitor one's commitments and one's chosen identity.

Conspicuously missing from this answer about baptism is any mention of God or the church in one's being baptized. The stress remains firmly on the actions and motivations of the individual, with the "power" of the ceremony coming from the choice of the person rather than any divine initiative. Hertzler gives no sense of the place of the community of faith in preparing and calling the candidate to baptism. In addition, the "strength" of the church here comes from *individuals* making the choice for a "Christ-centered life[style]," rather than the presence of the Holy Spirit within the congregation moving persons to the baptismal font. One can certainly applaud the emphasis on personally following Christ. Yet without acknowledging God's role in the process, Mennonite practice risks making baptism a purely human act.

Consider also the shift in the meaning and practice of foot washing, another Mennonite ecclesial practice. Keith Graber-Miller claims that the meaning of the rite has changed for Mennonites as their identity as a group has changed.[29] Mennonite theologizing has maintained the traditional interpretation that foot washing signifies both humble service and the need for cleansing from sin. Graber-Miller found that as the Mennonite Church shifted from a passive, withdrawn stance to a more activist one, the service theme of the rite eclipsed the notion of foot washing as an act of cleansing. This activist orientation is present in references to foot washing on the *Third Way Café* website. Of the scanty allusions to foot washing on the site, one does include a quote from the Dordrecht Confession about the ordinance being a cleansing from sin. Yet the service theme receives more attention. For example, Mennonites "observe footwashing because we believe that Jesus calls us to serve one another in love as he did. Foot washing becomes a symbolic act of service to one another."[30] Thus the prevalence of interpreting foot washing as service rather than receiving forgiveness or cleansing means that contemporary theologizing appears

---

29 Keith Graber-Miller, "Mennonite Footwashing: Identity Reflections and Altered Meanings," *Worship* 66, no. 2 (March 1992): 148–70.

30 Third Way Café website, "Rituals," accessed March 30, 2014. www.thirdway. com. Article 13 of the *Confession of Faith in a Mennonite Perspective* has a similar bias. The short article and commentary have seven references to service and just two regarding the theme of cleansing in regards to foot washing. General Conference Mennonite Church and Mennonite Church, *Confession of Faith in a Mennonite Perspective* (Scottdale, PA: Herald, 1995), 53–54. One also notices the predominance of the service theme by noting that one reference to cleansing is how *service* cleanses one from sin (54).

much more comfortable being foot wash*ers* rather than being the foot wash*ed*.[31] Certainly, the church can perform and interpret foot washing as a ritual of service. Yet questions arise when foot washing as an ordinance of *reception* has been virtually dropped from Mennonite theologizing and catechetical texts around the practice.

A Mennonite identity caught up with the choosing self appears much more comfortable building houses or taking care of others, rather than letting him- or herself be cared for. The image of a community of solitary heroes may appear to challenge the dominant story of consumer capitalism. Yet this picture still abides by the rules and narrative of the individualistic and subjective self. Mennonite practices need a more holistic and earthly likeness to truly counter the hold the reflexive self has on the Western moral imagination.

Christian Disciples as Dependent Creatures

If the fundamental orientation to life of the reflexive self is towards independence, the truthful anthropology of the Christian self begins with *dependence*. The Christian recognizes in Paul's speech in Athens the utter reliance she has on God for her fundamental existence: "In him we live and move and have our being" (Acts 17:28). The person of faith understands his dependence on God and others from birth to death and everything in between. Rather than being a sign of weakness in childhood or old age, or a temporary anomaly for the adult, believers acknowledge that an utter reliance on others for life is constitutive of the human condition. Christians recognize that the choosing self's belief in a self-originating and self-monitoring identity represents nothing less than a pernicious myth which erodes authentic human community. Christians acknowledge dependence as a fundamental truth of being humans created by God rather than gods creating their own reality.

Thus the primary identity of the Christian is that of being a *creature*, limited and fragile, yet created by a good God for a mission in the world. A creature knows that it does not make its own identity from the disenchanted raw mate-

---

31 For the emphasis on being foot washers, see the articles by Tripp York, "Dirty Basins, Dirty Disciples, and Beautiful Crosses: The Politics of Footwashing," *Liturgy* 20, no. 1 (February 2005): 13–15, and Mark Thiessen Nation's "Footwashing: Preparation for Christian Life," in *The Blackwell Companion to Christian Ethics*, eds. Stanley Hauerwas and Samuel Wells (Maldon, MA: Blackwell, 2nd edn, 2011), 479–90. For a critique of this view of foot washing using the thought of Jean Vanier, see Romand Coles, "'Gentled Into Being': Vanier and the Border at the Core," in eds. Stanley Hauerwas and Romand Coles, *Christianity, Democracy, and the Radical Ordinary: Conversations Between a Radical Democrat and a Christian* (Eugene, OR: Cascade, 2008), 208–28.

rials of the external environment, but understands its identity as a gift of grace. Without the grace of God pervading and invigorating all of life, all work and striving come to naught. So it goes with the church as well. "The Church is a community of those gathered not by choice but by grace," writes moral theologian Paul Wadell. "We are there only because God has summoned us in Christ . . . . [T]he crucial fact is that God's choice of us precedes and must govern our choice of one another. It is God acting through Christ who constitutes the community of faith, and it is God's action which shape and determine our own."[32] Knowledge never originates in the individual self, and Christian community never forms primarily around like-minded, voluntaristic individuals. Rather, the Trinity preveniently calls and invites believers into the divine life and into the body of Christ. No one lives, let alone survives, without being radically dependent on God and others for human flourishing.

Thus being a creature means understanding that people are created not to be independent, autonomous agents but dependent on one another.

> As Christians we know we have not been created to be 'our own authors,' to be autonomous. We are creatures. Dependency, not autonomy, is one of the ontological characteristics of our lives. That we are creatures, moreover, is but a reminder that we are created with and for one another. We are not just accidentally communal, but we are such by necessity. We are not created to be alone.[33]

Nothing could be more foreign for the Christian self than to believe that it alone builds and constructs its identity.

Because the Christian is created to live in community, she understands identity formation as a fundamentally *communal* exercise. A creature never becomes a self in isolation, but depends on the social recognition of others. The formation of identity is a dialogical rather than monological process, one in which the self is created just as much by the stories others tell about us as about the stories we choose and create.[34] The Christian knows herself to always

---

32 Paul J. Wadell, "Pondering the Anomaly of God's Love: Ethical Reflections on Access to the Sacraments," in *Developmental Disabilities and Sacramental Access: New Paradigms for Sacramental Encounters*, ed. Edward Foley (Collegeville, MN: Liturgical, 1994), 69.

33 Stanley Hauerwas, *Sanctify Them in the Truth: Holiness Exemplified* (Nashville, TN: Abingdon, 1998), 147.

34 "None of us really tells or owns our stories. We are all people who are storied by a Creator God who resides within a narrative of creation, cross, and redemption that we can share in but can never own." Swinton, Mowat and Baines, "Whose Story Am I?", 11.

belong to a broader story due to her dependence as a creature. Not only does the believer understand herself as a part of the story of Jesus, but also acknowledges that that story means nothing outside the community which attempts to embody it on a daily basis.

A continual state of vulnerability accompanies the Christian's dependence on God and others. While the reflexive self only sees vulnerability as an obstacle to the successful pursuit of its life plan, the believer understands fragility as not only being a part of his creatureliness but also as the mode which makes him *available for relationship* with the other. As the seventeenth-century Christian theologian and mystic Thomas Traherne evocatively suggests, "Wants are the bands and cements between God and us . . . the ligatures . . . the sinews that convey senses from Him into us, whereby we live in Him and feel His enjoyments."[35] The presence of the other represents life for Christians, because without others life and flourishing cannot occur. As Jesus welcomed humanity into the divine community through calling them friends, so must believers extend that same hosting to others. Christians understand hospitality not as throwing dinner parties but of a copious welcome of the stranger, the same welcome they received as creatures from a welcoming God.

The limitations which come from creaturely vulnerability train the believer in learning how to receive grace and the gift of the other. Late modernity's bias towards self-construction demands a self always and everywhere in control of its life plan, ready to use the givens of life to further its goals of self-fulfillment. Feminist philosopher Soran Reader sees this bias as a truncation of human being, and believes that "patiency" as much as agency defines the human person. Reader suggests that:

> passivity, inability, necessity/contingency and dependency are as constitutive of personhood as the 'positive' aspects of action, capability, choice and independence which according to the agential conception are necessary and sufficient for personhood on their own. Along with agency comes patiency. Along with capabilities, come inabilities. Along with freedom, choice, and rationality come constraint, necessity and contingency. And along with independence come dependencies.[36]

While the late modern choosing self stumbles at the seemingly severe restraints

---

On identity being a "dialogical process," see Charles Taylor, "The Politics of Recognition," in *Multiculturalism: Examining the Politics of Recognition*, ed. Amy Gutman (Princeton, NJ: Princeton University Press, 1994), 33–34.

35 Thomas Traherne, *Centuries*, I.51 (London: Mowbray, 1985), 24.

36 Soran Reader, "The Other Side of Agency," *Philosophy* 82, no. 322 (October 2007): 592.

of patiency, the Christian creature knows the "other side of agency" as self-evident truth. Receptivity and openness to the grace of God in others and the world stand as fundamental markers of creaturely identity.

What creatures wait for and receive are not disconnected spirits but living, breathing, vulnerable *bodies*. The reflexive self can easily live alone inside its own life plans and pursuits of rational desire, remaining oblivious to how bodies need others to truly flourish. "A mortal body is a dependent being," writes John Dunnill. "If I think of my *self* as a mind or a spirit, I may think that I am self-sustaining, without needs; but as a *body* I need people."[37] Creatures recognize the needs of others through their own need, and thus do not thoughtlessly buy from a disembodied brand but seek some connection with the bodies behind the product.

In addition, Christians know that bodies are not mere raw material for identity construction, but are gifts from a good, Creator God. Learning how to receive their bodies as gifts trains creatures in how to suffer those contingencies of life which cannot be eliminated or ameliorated. Rather than seeing bodily imperfections merely as defects for modification or removal, creatures know how to patiently accompany and suffer with the other without needing to eliminate the sufferer. For example, a Christian who recognizes the inherent limitations of creaturely life can discern in a (potential) person with Down's syndrome not a "genetic abnormality" but a precious gift of a loving Creator. To identify oneself as a dependent being means knowing that bodies need other bodies, and that God has created a church abounding in difference and diversity (1 Cor. 12).

Furthermore, when Christians realize how fundamental dependence is to true human being and flourishing, they also realize that the real moral exemplars of creatureliness are much different than the heroes promulgated by the choosing self. In a church of mutual dependence, people with disabilities or other unalterable limitations become not defectives but potential *teachers* in what it might mean truthfully to own Christian identity. The church needs communities like L'Arche and Word Made Flesh, who have discovered that the vulnerable stand less as objects of charity than as potential friends of wisdom and humanity.[38] These communities have discovered that the choosing self, hell-bent on independence and control, can never truly flourish because it lives a lie. Only as dependent bodies utterly reliant on God, one another, and the

---

37 John Dunnill, "Being a Body," *Theology* 105, no. 824 (March 1, 2002): 112.

38 For more on the international federation of L'Arche communities, see www.larche.org. Information on Word Made Flesh can be found at www.wordmadeflesh.org.

planet can humanity receive the grace to understand authentic human identity.

Communities like L'Arche reveal a Christian truth: that all identity must be grounded in the knowledge that no one is independent, but fundamentally belongs to the Other. Theologian John Swinton states it eloquently:

> In a very real sense we belong to one another; I am because we are . . . . We need to belong before we can understand the true meaning of such things as autonomy, freedom, and self-representation. When we belong to the Christian community the true meaning of these terms becomes quite clear: in Jesus there is no autonomy, freedom or self-representation. We are slaves to Jesus (1 Cor 7:22). Autonomy is a cultural illusion; person-hood emerges from gift and relationship; creation and friendship; freedom comes from enslavement to Jesus and self-representation emerges as we learn what it means to live out and live within the image of God: Jesus. It is as we learn what it means to give up or at least to reframe these culturally important social goods, that we learn what it means truly to be human and to create the types of community wherein humanness can be actualized.[39]

Christian creatures see through the seductions of the You Sell as cultural illusions which deny the truth that relationships rather than self-representation represent true human goods. Disciples live out of an identity defined by Jesus, and thus depend on the Trinity for all self-definition.

Practicing a True Christian Creaturely Identity

Conceptions of human identity never remain merely abstract ideas, but inevitably become embodied in practices. This article has shown how recent popular theologizing and praxis around the Mennonite sacramental practices of foot washing and baptism potentially cohere too neatly with the late modern reflexive self. While the intention behind these ordinances may desire to act as an alternative to the excesses of late consumer capitalism, its subjectivistic and individualistic tendencies potentially dull its efficacy as a counter-narrative.

The following are tentative suggestions on how Mennonite sacramental practices might be renewed, reimagined, and reinvigorated to more faithfully witness to the gospel and Christian identity. By paying more attention to God's initiative in the ordinances, recognizing the church as subject in the community's ritual activity, and recovering the body in worship, Mennonites might become formed into dependent creatures given to the world as witnesses of Christ's peace.

---

39 John Swinton, "From Inclusion to Belonging: A Practical Theology of Community, Disability and Humanness," *Journal of Religion, Disability & Health* 16, no. 2 (April 2012): 184.

Reemphasizing God's initiative in ecclesial practices

Christians attuned to creaturely life acknowledge that all of life is utterly dependent on God, and that the church is not merely a voluntaristic gathering of like-minded individuals but a body called into being by God. Believers thus understand themselves not fundamentally as choosers or makers but as *receivers* of God's grace. As Mennonite theologian Irma Fast Dueck explains, in worship:

> we discover our identity lies not primarily in the culture from which we come, the family into which we were born, or the church denomination that shaped us: our identity lies in the Trinity – in God through Jesus Christ and as revealed by the Holy Spirit. In worship we discover who by the grace of God we are, and who we are meant to be. This is an identity we do not earn or achieve or create, but receive as a gift.[40]

With God as actor, the human role in the ordinance concerns itself less with what it needs to do than what it needs to receive. Reemphasizing the priority of God's action not only might help curb a Mennonite tendency towards self-originated activism, but also coheres with the robust pneumatology of the first Radical Reformers. A common element in the thought and practice of sixteenth-century Anabaptists was the crucial place the Holy Spirit had in conversion, the preparation for baptism, and for Christian life as a whole.[41]

When Christians acknowledge God as first and primary actor, they know that they never name themselves but are fundamentally named by God and by others in the body. Sacramental practices emanate as modes of God's grace, transforming persons from autonomous monads into friends belonging to Christ and the church. Joel Shuman and Keith Meador go on to say that worship reminds Christians "that their lives are no longer their own, but gifts from God to be received as such . . . . [Baptism] embodies a narrative of reception, witness, and sharing with a full acknowledgement of our utter dependence on the other for our present communion as well as our eschatological vision of hope for the future."[42]

A focus on baptism as an act of God first and foremost challenges the

---

40 Irma Fast Dueck, "Worship Made Strange," in *The Church Made Strange for the Nations*, eds. Paul G. Doerksen and Karl Koop (Eugene, OR: Pickwick, 2011), 116.

41 Thus writes Pilgram Marpeck, "Without the artistry and teaching of the Holy Spirit, who pours out the love, which is God, into the hearts of the faith, and which surpasses all reason and understanding, everything is in vain." Quoted in Roth, *Practices*, 204.

42 Keith G. Meador and Joel James Shuman, "Who/se We Are: Baptism as Personhood," *Christian Bioethics* 6, no. 1 (April 2000): 79.

choosing self, who believes that it can make its own life. Rather, when the church stresses the Holy Spirit as agent of grace in the ordinance, Christians remember that believers are all created and continually being created by God in total gratuity and care. Foot washing has the potential to reveal this aspect of grace in a powerful way by emphasizing that Christians cannot wash themselves but must be washed by another. Foot washing embodies humanity's reliance on God and one another for the recognition of the gift of their lives. In learning to have their feet washed, Christians recognize the power of the Holy Spirit in gratuitously (re-)creating persons into the people of God.

Recovering the church as the primary subject of Mennonite practices

Dependent creatures know that the reflexive self's rejection of social institutions as constraints on freedom merely pushes people further into the organizational domain of late consumer capitalism. Truthful Christian identity requires belonging to and participating in the body of Christ. According to Stanley Hauerwas, "We require practices through which we learn that we do not know who we are, or what our bodies can and cannot do, until we are told what and who we are by a more determinative 'body.'"[43]

Thus practices like baptism and foot washing produce not merely individual believers but a *community* of faith. The church does not consist of atomized selves but of a new social reality which changes and becomes more the body of Christ every time sacramental practices are performed. Recognizing the church as a subject in Mennonite practices coheres with the original impulses of the sixteenth-century movement. The solid and robust ecclesiology of the Radical Reformers could not conceive of the mere contractual gathering of individuals believed by the choosing self. Instead, it recognized the church as the Body of Christ in which individuals never believed alone but always in communion with one another.

This communion means that faith consists not in a perpetual monitoring of one's inner motivations and allegiance to God, but requires a community which can remember God when the individual forgets. It should come as no surprise that a condition like dementia strikes fear into the heart of the reflexive self. When a successful life plan demands a continual knowing what one is doing, the prospect of forgetting can only mean the death of the self. Yet when the church performs sacramental practices not as individuals but as a body, it trains Christians in seeing that even though one may forget, the body remembers

---

43 Stanley Hauerwas, *In Good Company: The Church as Polis* (Notre Dame, IN: University of Notre Dame Press, 1995), 24.

through the performance of rituals like foot washing and baptism.[44] A Christian identity as dependent creatures affirms that a Christian faith cannot exist in isolation but must be in relation with others. Just as our faith never wholly originates with us but comes as a gift from God, so our faith must never be only for us but for the church, God's people.

Paying attention to the body

Anecdotal evidence suggests that at least a significant minority of people express concern at the highly cerebral dimension of worship in Mennonite congregations. Mennonites have inherited an anti-sacramental orientation which served as a corrective to medieval abuses, but has also often failed to recognize how praise and thanksgiving require not just minds but also *bodies*. At the same time, a burgeoning choosing self feels quite comfortable leaving matters to an inner subjectivity, whether that be in matters of worship or self-fulfillment. The combination of these two tendencies means that bodies are important when they break down and need to be repaired or modified, but otherwise life and faith primarily center in the head.

The Christian living out of an identity of creatureliness understands life as fundamentally a *bodily* life, and that the practices of the church form and train the body into a cruciform shape. Believers recognize faith not primarily as a state of mind but as a bodily practice, a trust that the body knows and performs before the intellect grasps. Communion in the body of Christ is not one of disembodied minds pursuing their own life plans, but of bodies called by the Trinity into communities of faith.

Mennonite pastor Isaac Villegas writes eloquently on the centrality of the body in the practice of foot washing. On his experience of letting his feet be washed by an older African American man, Villegas relates how "I didn't say anything. I just sat there, submissive, receptive, letting him take me, my feet, into him, his hands — a moment of union, our union in the body of Christ. God's revolution happens when you let someone take your dirty feet in her hands, because with those hands comes Christ's love."[45] The self-evident nature of the body in the rite revealed to Villegas how dependent Christians are on God and one another. Foot washing is a "practice that breaks down walls of

---

44 For an excellent attempt to "re-describe" dementia in the Christian community, see John Swinton's *Dementia: Living in the Memories of God* (Grand Rapids, MI: Eerdmans, 2012).

45 Isaac Villegas, "A Holy Hybridity: Reflections on a Footwashing Service," *The Mennonite*, April 2, 2012, accessed March 23, 2014. www.themennonite.org/issues/15-4/articles/A_Holy_Hybridity.

self-sufficiency and opens us to receive God's loving care from another."[46] This nonviolent care of one another needs not the surgical modifications of bio-medicine nor the product customizations of the You Sell. Instead, dependent creatures know that all that is needed is a community of faith, and the towel and basin which can make enemies friends and create a peaceable witness to the world. "Jesus didn't tell us to wash our own feet but to wash each other's feet. For in letting someone wash our feet, we draw closer to our fundamental neediness; God's sustaining grace washes over us."[47] Recognizing dependency lets the body be the body, rather than the perpetual project for the reflexive self. In baptism and foot washing, letting those bodies be creates a body from which Christ is witnessed to the world.

Incorporating more liturgical gestures within Mennonite worship could assist in training members how to be authentic Christian creatures. Worship is a fundamentally *communal* activity which requires *bodies* that give praise and thanksgiving to God. By paying attention to liturgical gestures within worship, Mennonite Christians let their bodies communicate their thanks to God and receive God's love in return. At the same time, they also affirm that they can never truly know God on their own. Just as bodies cannot survive long on their own, so Christian identity centered around independence and self-sufficiency remains truncated and wholly insufficient. The Christian self is nothing less than a body within a body.

Conclusion

This article argues that the reflexive self of late modernity untruthfully promulgates and practices an identity of the human as an independent chooser. The ever alterable self of contemporary Western liberalism leaves persons suspicious of the givenness of human contingency, while also training them in the practices of consumer capitalism like cosmetic surgery and the You Sell. Recent theologizing around Mennonite practices reveals a highly subjectivistic and agency driven self, potentially mirroring too closely the excesses of the late modern social imaginary. This turn to a more independent self risks eclipsing the Radical Reformers' belief in the prevenience of God's action for the Christian life, and thus threatens to alienate Mennonites from the font of ethical action they seek to emulate.

---

46 Isaac Villegas, "Sheeplike Love: Grace and Truth — A Word from Pastors," *The Mennonite*, April 1, 2011, accessed March 23, 2014. www.themennonite.org/issues/14-4/articles/Sheeplike_love.

47 Villegas, "Sheeplike Love."

A turn to a more dependent and creaturely identity stands as a potential alternative witness to the dominance of the reflexive self. Increasingly incomprehensible to a late modern world held captive by the vision of the autonomous individual, the Christian acknowledges her fundamental need for God and others for her very being. Human contingency represents not an impediment to the moral life, but the font of true human flourishing where patience and receptivity lead to a communion of bodies in a Body. The Mennonite sacramental practices of baptism and foot washing offer training grounds for supporting this kind of theological anthropology. By reimaging and returning to a more truthful identity as dependent creatures of the living God, Mennonites might offer a bold witness to a world intolerant of those unable to speak for themselves. And by so doing, Anabaptists could not only serve the poor but also learn from those disqualified others the power of God who brings a peace the world cannot give.

The Hokkaido Confession of Faith and Mission in Japanese Context

YOSHIHIRO KOBAYASHI[1]

Introduction

This article is written in response to the critical situation we are facing in Japan, where the ongoing nuclear catastrophe in Fukushima is still far from settled, and invisible radioactive substances are destroying the beautiful creation of God. A change in our peace-oriented constitution has become much more likely under the leadership of Prime Minister Shinzo Abe and his Liberal Democratic party. The party's proposed draft of a revised constitution would make the emperor the head of state, set up a national defense force, and permit the right of collective self-defense to be exercised.

According to Scripture, life is the most precious gift from God and he commanded that we should choose this gift instead of death.[2] It is this same life that is being threatened in a wide range of dimensions in Japan, and perhaps equally in other countries. We must think seriously about what it means to be a Christian and to follow the footsteps of Jesus Christ in today's world. The newly adopted Hokkaido Confession of Faith is a reflection of this attempt to follow Jesus today. It expresses an understanding of mission from a Japanese context, but many believe firmly that this confession will be of benefit to fellow Christians facing similar difficulties elsewhere. It is our hope that we are faithful to the good news of Jesus Christ, and the mission of God to bring about peace and justice, and, with the leading of the Holy Spirit, to combine our efforts so that we may be called children of God.

Hokkaido is in the northern part of Japan and is the second largest of four main islands in this country. Mennonite missionary work began here in 1951. There are eighteen Mennonite churches in the Japan Mennonite Christian Church Conference, with a combined membership of approximately 450. The conference has two centers for reinforcing Anabaptist–Mennonite core values,

---

1 *Yoshihiro Kobayashi is a Mennonite minister in Sapporo and also a physician at a hospice for cancer patients. He is a director of the Mennonite Education and Research Center in Hokkaido Conference and a Board member of the multireligious Hokkaido Council of Religions for Peace.*

2 Deut. 30:15–20, Ps. 72:13–14, John 1:1–5; Rom. 8:2.

namely the values of the fellowship of believers, discipleship, and the peace witness. The Peace and Mission Center provides an annual seminar on various social and missiological issues. The Mennonite Education and Research Center provides various lectures and seminars on theology, Anabaptist studies, and biblical studies. It also publishes a quarterly newsletter called Kakehashi ("The Bridgebuilder"), which has served the fellowship among Anabaptist denominations in Japan for more than twenty-five years.

Japan Mennonite Christian Church Conference (Hokkaido) Confession of Faith

Adopted by the 61st General Conference of the Japan Mennonite Christian Church Conference, May 18, 2013[3]

The Japan Mennonite Christian Church Conference is a people of God, a community of the Lord, and in the Anabaptist–Mennonite faith tradition that began in the sixteenth-century Reformation. Congregations in the conference cooperatively share in the work of evangelization. Each congregation is autonomous, independent, and self-supporting, but as disciples of Jesus Christ we hereby establish the Japan Mennonite Christian Church Conference Confession of Faith to reaffirm our shared faith today with the hope of further deepening our mutual fellowship and cooperation.

The Lord Jesus Christ is at the center of our confession of faith. The Lord preached the good news of the kingdom of God, walked the way of the cross, and through his teaching, his life, and his death, he redeemed us from sin and calls us to be disciples. The risen Lord defeated death and is at work ahead of us even today. We follow this Jesus Christ, to which the Old and New Testament give testimony, as our sole savior and sole role model for our faith and life, and we worship God the Father of Jesus Christ.

We are a branch of the worldwide body of Mennonite churches. With this in mind, we join our Mennonite brothers and sisters in confessing the "Shared Convictions" statement (adopted by the Mennonite World Conference General Council in March 2006).[4] This expresses the faith that unites Anabaptist–Mennonites who walk in the path of the disciples in today's world.

We are also a branch of the people of God, and separated into various churches around the world. Remembering this, we join all brothers and sisters

---

3 This is an official translation confirmed by the conference. Ken Johnson Shenk translated it at the request of the Mennonite Education and Research Center.

4 "Shared Convictions" was adopted by Mennonite World Conference General Council, Pasadena, California (USA), March 15, 2006.

in confessing the creeds of the worldwide church, starting with the Apostles' Creed.[5]

The Lord Jesus Christ will one day come to make all things new. We have been granted imperishable hope. As we wait for that day, we live, work, and strive to faithfully walk in the path of the Lord's gospel. Protect us, O Lord, and guide us.

This we believe:

1. Jesus Christ is the Word of God the Father, and is revealed by the Holy Spirit.
2. The church is a community of believers which learns from the Bible under the guidance of the Holy Spirit.
3. Believers listen to the Lord Jesus Christ, serve each other, and love their neighbors.
4. Believers care for creation, build peace and justice which come from Christ, and participate in the work of the Kingdom of God.
5. Following Jesus' nonviolent way of life, we as believers do not participate in war.

Reflections on the Confession of Faith

In 2013, the Japan Mennonite Christian Church Conference adopted its first confession of faith in over sixty years of mission history. Although the Mennonite population, including several Anabaptist denominations, is not very large and is a minority within the Christian minority in this country, we are confident that the Anabaptist–Mennonite faith tradition can make an indispensable contribution to the efforts of witness and service of the entire Japanese Christian body. Particular ways in which the Anabaptist–Mennonite tradition can contribute include: holding the lordship of Jesus Christ against the worldly principalities and powers, in underscoring a costly obedience to Jesus Christ our Lord; and in proclaiming peace and justice according to the good news of the kingdom of God. In this short article I will review the theological impli-

---

5 "Creeds of the worldwide church" is a term used in the Western church tradition to refer to the Nicene Creed, the Apostles' Creed, the Chalcedonian Creed, and the Athanasian Creed. It also refers to ecumenical creeds or universal creeds. These creeds are accepted by almost all Christian denominations in the Western and Eastern church traditions. Though the Eastern Orthodox Church doesn't use the Apostles' Creed and the Athanasian Creed in its liturgy, the contents of both creeds have never been denied in its history.

cations of the confession, as well as its significance to the mission and witness of Christian churches in the Japanese setting. We can summarize the basic characteristics of the confession as follows:

1. Following Jesus Christ as the central component of the Anabaptist–Mennonite faith tradition is clearly represented in this confession. Keeping the Christian faith means obeying the Lord Jesus daily, seeking for and living in the kingdom of God and his justice, and loving God and our neighbors.
2. This basic line of faith is observed by reading the Scriptures repeatedly under the guidance of the Holy Spirit, which is the spirit of Jesus Christ, and listening carefully to his voice in the congregation. This assignment is not just for ministers or pastors, but is a crucial ministry for every Christian in every fellowship.
3. Our confession avoids use of doctrinal words and phrases as much as possible, rather designating several guidelines for our Christian life. Doctrine has caused disputes and brought disunity and divisions among Anabaptist–Mennonites, as well as in the entire Christian church. Our unity is not built on dogma or doctrine, but on the firm foundation of Jesus Christ and obedient life in service to him.
4. The way of nonviolence is explicitly stated in our confession, which is rarely seen in other Christian traditions. This is an essential statement for our Christian witness and obedience.

Strongly emphasizing the lordship of Jesus Christ, this confession places him at the center, and this is indicated in its second paragraph. If this lordship of Jesus Christ is disregarded, the Christian church can incur the disastrous consequences of its own unbelief. In 1967, the largest Protestant denomination in Japan, the United Church of Christ (*Kyodan*), publicized the Confession on the Responsibility During World War II.[6] It says with deep regret:

> The church, as "the light of the world" and as "the salt of the earth," should not have aligned itself with that war effort. Love of country should, rather, have led Christians to exercise a rightful judgment, based on Christian

---

6 Protestant churches in Japan originated from the work of foreign missionaries who came to Japan in 1859. Subsequently denominations from Europe and America were transplanted to Japan, and their mission work expanded. Proposals for union arose frequently among the several denominations, partly stimulated from abroad by the ecumenical movement, but ironically this union was implemented by the Religious Organizations Law in June, 1941.

conscience, toward the course our nation pursued. However, in the name of the *Kyodan*, we issued a statement at home and abroad in which we approved of and supported that war, and encouraged prayers for victory.[7]

Since the formation of the United Church of Christ in Japan, itself deeply connected with the militaristic government and its policy of advocating war, the *Kyodan* could not bear a faithful witness for peace and justice. Before World War II, an alliance of countries centered around Japan, Germany, and Italy, forming the Axis of Powers. During this period, an historic *Kirchenkampf* ("church struggle") was fought by the Confessing Church against government-sponsored efforts to Nazify the German Protestant church. It was Karl Barth who played a predominant role in the struggle, and his work was well read by the leading *Kyodan* theologians at that time.[8] His series of *Church Dogmatics* were highly recommended for theological studies and lectured on in the *Kyodan* seminaries, but his notable contribution in the struggle was completely ignored as if the Barmen Declaration against the Nazi and heretic German Christian movement did not exist.[9] These *Kyodan* theologians who admired Barth kept silent, or even aggressively supported the war that was driven by Japanese militarism and the Absolutistic Emperor System.[10] Their silence and support illustrates how Christian faith and theology can experience intellectual

---

This law was made after Nazi Germany's Gleichschaltung or "forcible-coordination" policy by the Japanese militaristic government. The law forced all the Protestant denominations to unite into one church body, the United Church of Christ in Japan (Kyodan) and to cooperate with the government and its policy of advocating war. The Kyodan had been under government control since Japan's defeat in 1945.

7 "The Confession on the Responsibility During World War II of the United Church of Christ in Japan (*Kyodan*)" was approved by the Kyodan Executive Committee, February 20, 1967, and issued on Easter Sunday, March 26, 1967. This citation is from the Revised English Translation issued on January 20, 1982. Accessed April 10, 2014. http://uccj-e.org/confession

8 The influence of Karl Barth upon Japanese Protestant theologians began in early 1920s, particularly among those who were not satisfied with both the predominant liberal theology and a newly developing fundamentalism. For these theologians, the former seemed too optimistic about human reality and powerless to sinful reality in the world, and the latter seemed irrational and ignorant. Neo-orthodoxy, or Barth's theology of the Word, soon became an influential alternative to both.

9 *Church Dogmatics (Kirchliche Dogmatik)* is the thirteen-volume unfinished major work of Karl Barth. It was published in stages from 1932 to 1967.

10 From the Meiji Restoration in 1868 to the defeat of Imperial Japan in 1945, Japan was under the rule of the emperor's despotism (Absolutistic Emperor System). Under the regime, the people were deprived of civil rights and liberties;

deterioration without obedience to Jesus Christ. Christian faith can be Christian only in discipleship and on the way to the cross. The centrality of Jesus Christ is a touchstone of the Christian faith and theology. Without this notion, the mission of the church itself can easily degenerate into heresy.

This exclusive character of Christian faith, in which only Jesus Christ is worshipped and obeyed, paradoxically contains a radical inclusiveness in its nature. In Matthew 8:5–13, Jesus proposed to a Roman centurion that he would go to the Roman military camp to save his servant. The story is astonishing, mainly because of the chosen conversation partner, but also because of the place where Jesus is willing to go. The action Jesus proposes could have caused a furious response from the Jews, but Jesus doesn't seem to consider this. If we take seriously Jesus' radical inclusiveness, and become willing to heal and visit even our enemies, the church's focus will no longer remain on doctrinal disputes.

In the course of the adoption of our confession, there appeared a repeated criticism from a conservative or fundamental circle in our churches that issues of Christian doctrine should be added to the confession, such as on original sin or vicarious atonement. But it is crucially important for Christians to make clear that the ultimate norm of biblical interpretation is Jesus Christ himself, rather than doctrine. The Christian creeds and confessions are called *norma normata* (a rule that is ruled), while the Bible is called *norma normans* (the rule that rules), but we can affirm that Jesus himself is the sole *norma normans* for all Christian thinking and action. God's call to his people is to serve others in need both materially and spiritually, not to judge each other over the subjects of Christian doctrine. Our unity should be built on the firm foundation of Jesus Christ, not on doctrine.

Implications for the Japanese Context

Since the start of the Abe Administration in 2012, the political and military tensions in Northeast Asia have continued to intensify. The Japanese government seems to give priority to policy that supports building up its military power instead of seeking peace and reconciliation in this region. Additionally, the government is zealous for the constitutional amendment described above, and to resume nuclear power plant operations, despite the strong opposition of citizens.

---

the semi-feudal landlord system, which squeezed tenant peasants into paying heavy rents, prevailed in rural areas. The present Constitution of Japan came into effect in 1947. The constitution established the people's sovereignty, renunciation of war, fundamental human rights, the National Diet as the supreme state organ, local autonomy, and a series of other democratic and peaceful provisions that serve as pillars of democracy.

The essential ministry of the Christian church is to serve the mission of God. This is the very reason the church exists. As a people of God, we are called to be a faithful servant for God's mission. In *Transforming Mission: Paradigm Shifts in Theology of Mission*, David Bosch says that "there is church because there is mission, not vice versa . . . To participate in mission is to participate in the movement of God's love toward people, since God is a fountain of sending love."[11] Bosch continues:

> The primary purpose of the *missiones ecclesiae* can therefore not simply be the planting of churches or the saving of souls; rather, it has to be service to the *missio Dei*, representing God in and over against the world, pointing to God, holding up the God-child before the eyes of the world in a ceaseless celebration of the Feast of the Epiphany. In its mission, the church witnesses to the fullness of the promise of God's reign and participates in the ongoing struggle between that reign and the powers of darkness and evil.[12]

Thus the missionary task of the Christian church is not about self-extension, but fundamentally is about active participation in radical witness against principalities and powers that are embodied in various forms of evil — including in socioeconomic, political, and military dimensions.

During World War II, the Japanese Christians committed a grave mistake in obeying structural evils, which led this and neighboring countries to destruction. The only way to avoid such a mistake again is to listen to the Lord Jesus Christ, serve each other, and love our neighbors (article 3 of the Confession of Faith). We must follow him faithfully, even to the point of radical inclusiveness. Maintaining this stance, we seek the *shalom* of God, and might overcome our internal theological conflicts that cause division. Moreover, we might even serve as a catalyst, inspiring the people in Northeast Asia to mutual understanding and reconciliation.

---

11 David J. Bosch, *Transforming Mission: Paradigm Shifts in Theology of Mission* (Orbis Books, 1991), 390.

12 Ibid., 391.

The Shenandoah Confession:

A Critical Introduction to the Next Generation

EVAN K. M. KNAPPENBERGER[1]

Occupy Anabaptism: A Prelude

When I joined the Charlottesville, Virginia, chapter of the Occupy Wall Street protest nearly three years ago, I was already an accomplished activist with Veterans for Peace, deeply committed to the cause and mission of social justice in light of the prophetic calling. Unfortunately, many of the young people called by the Spirit to our Occupy Charlottesville encampment had no real background in the countercultural work which we were trying to do, and many of their good intentions fell on rocky ground and there they withered in the sun, lacking a deep rootedness. The problem most modern Anabaptists face, whether they are aware of it or not, is precisely the opposite: having found the fertile ground, the many and large branches of various Mennonite and Amish sects grow — but often these branches bear little or dubious fruit, feeding only ethnic enclaves or myopic communities and ignoring the hard work of the Spirit that is demanded of Christians in the world.[2]

At one Occupy Charlottesville press conference that fall — in Robert E. Lee Park under a giant statue of that icon of the failure of violence to deliver the people of Central Virginia — I presented a homily citing Christian ethics and Hebrew Scripture. My tiny attempt to connect social justice to religious

---

1 *Evan K. M. Knappenberger is a philosophy and theology student at Eastern Mennonite University, and President of Chapter 171 of Veterans for Peace. He studies with and would like to thank Nancy Heisey, Ted Grimsrud, Christian Early, Peter Dula, and Linford Stutzman.*

2 This is a sensitive topic, hitting a nerve in the Anabaptist community. It is not our intention here to explore the myopic psychologies of the purity ethic, but one example I would offer of this comes from a statement made by Dr. Vincent Harding in a recent interview with Dr. Mark Sawin about his work with Mennonites on behalf of Dr. King and the civil rights movement in the 1960s: "There was a sense sometimes, I remember, of being concerned that too often, too much Mennonite thought was being given as to how to have the cleanest hands, personally, and not how to do the largest work that needed to be done." (For more on this see: Evan Knappenberger, "Non-Resistance, Civil Rights and Mennonite Identity," *The Weather Vane* (March 23, 2014): sec. Features.)

truth resonated with some portions of the community, but surprised many of the young anarchist comrades who felt betrayed that I had been "a secret Christian among us this whole time." The feeling among the dispossessed youth — that they were doing something completely new and unheard-of by feeding the poor, housing the homeless, and educating the public — is stark evidence of the failure of the Christian project. While nearby congregations busied themselves with musical programming, capital improvement budgets, and doctrinal arguments, a bunch of grungy secular kids were out doing the hard work of Christ at all hours of day and night. And when the inevitable confrontations with authority came calling, still the good Christians were absent. No wonder then that the anarchist caucus was so eager to denigrate anyone self-identifying as Christian!

I know now, thanks to my friend and professor Dr. Ted Grimsrud, that there is, embedded in the Mennonite tradition, a deep understanding of the issues we struggled with at Occupy Charlottesville. Questions of authority and power are not new to Anabaptism. Despite the similarities of the Occupy Charlottesville and Mennonite ideologies, there was however no interface between the Occupiers and Anabaptism during my time with Occupy. When we desperately needed the theo-poetic guidance of prophetic awareness to liberate us from the poverty of authority-awareness the people who have been doing this for thousands of years were nowhere to be found.[3]

The quest for right relationships among human beings — the work of wholeness, shalom, and justice — cuts to the heart of what it means to engage the world in the spirit of Christ. The responsibility of those claiming the mantle of the prophetic calling is manifold, and carries implications for the future of the Anabaptist tradition. How should Anabaptists approach justice and nonviolence in a world where fruitless branches will be thrown into the fire?[4] For indeed the whole world has been set on fire.[5] Furthermore, there is absolutely no safety in embodying the "quiet in the land" — in fact the very future of the land itself is jeopardized with the ascendency of ecocide-capitalism and thermonuclear "security."[6]

---

3 I am blending elements of John Caputo, Peter Rollins, Walter Brueggemann, John Howard Yoder, and Walter Wink.

4 John 15.

5 Gospel of Thomas (10): Jesus said, "I have cast fire upon the world, and see, I am guarding it until it blazes." Also, Luke 12: 49.

6 According to some scientists, the worst climate-change projections may endanger even the existence of bacteria on Earth. For more on the paradigm-shifting nature of the crisis, see Derrick Jensen, *Endgame* (New York: Seven Stories Press, 2006).

How then should we act as Occupiers, as Anabaptists? What is left to the prophetic imagination in a time of hypermodernism, where personal connection happens on a Facebook screen, where blogging is considered working for social justice, and where ministry effectiveness is measured in "likes" and "+1's"? The metaphors we have used to understand the place of the church in civilization for thousands of years have collapsed; the desolating sacrilege of the idolatry of violence remains unchallenged in the mainstream.[7] And yet, remnants of the tradition of social justice — including many of the good-hearted Occupiers — still proliferate like weeds in the cracks of the social order, thirsting for the life-giving waters of the homeless activist and Lamb of God, Jesus of Nazareth.

How shall we speak to them, these unhappy anarchists, these traumatized Veterans for Peace, these agnostic university peacebuilding majors, these dropouts sleeping in strangers' tents in the cold October rain, shivering for justice and hungering for righteousness? How can we invite the transforming Spirit into our lives? How can we invite it into Zuccoti Park, the jury room and the frat house? How can we enter into the priesthood of believers with all these brothers and sisters? Can we find a common gospel language with which to communicate that good news given to us with joy? What experiential potential waits patiently to assert its forgotten quiet wisdom?

The way Anabaptists approach these questions in the coming years will determine the future of our institutions, the future of the faith, and also the future of the Earth itself. There is nothing less than the priesthood of all believers and the New Jerusalem at stake here — if we actually believe the message of the one who sends us, that is.

The Shenandoah Confession of Faith: An Introduction

In February of 2014, the Anabaptist student organization known as Intercollegiate Peace Fellowship held its annual conference at Eastern Mennonite Seminary in the beautiful Shenandoah Valley, Harrisonburg, Virginia. Students from seven institutions came together for a weekend of fellowship led by Center for Justice and Peacebuilding research professor Dr. Lisa Schirch, who works around the globe on issues of human security and nonviolent conflict transformation. In her opening address titled "A Tribe Called Mennonite," Schirch spoke about the foundations of Anabaptist faith, the Schleitheim-an-

---

7 See Ted Grimsrud, *Instead of Atonement the Bible's Salvation Story and Our Hope for Wholeness* (Eugene, OR: Cascade Books, 2013), or Walter Wink, *Engaging the Powers: Discernment and Resistance in a World of Domination* (Philadelphia, PA: Fortress Press, 1992).

der-Raden Confession of Faith of 1527,[8] and summarized five hundred years of Mennonite peacemaking.

Schirch then called participants to speak boldly of their beliefs, each contributing to a Shenandoah confession of faith. Participants in the conference then spent much of the next three days working in groups to define a draft confession of faith in order to better reflect values central to the Anabaptist paradigm. At the end of the conference, a committee was formed of Eastern Mennonite University students including Aaron Erb, Jacob Landis, Christine Baer, Krista Nyce, Chaska Yoder, myself, and a few EMU faculty and others attending the conference from other Mennonite organizations. Together over the course of several weeks, we struggled with theological language until finally, on the 487th anniversary of the publishing of Schleitheim, we released our document to the world.[9]

The final draft of the Shenandoah Confession of Faith surprised many, including members of the drafting committee. The language used in the document is theological and relational, uncompromising in the scope of its ecclesiastic endeavor, and somewhat avoids the language of secular theory. It is above all not something typical of twenty-year-old college students struggling through the doldrums of hypermodernity. This is one of the Shenandoah Confession's many strengths, and lives in the prophecy of Joel: "I will pour out my Spirit on all people. Your sons and daughters will prophesy . . ."[10]

The eleven articles of confession stand as monuments to the deep belief of those of us called to do the work of the Spirit. This is no idolatry of belief, no shallow self-justification by faith alone; the articles of the Shenandoah Confession, like the articles of Schleitheim, are not meant to be mere poetics. The Shenandoah Confession is no Augustinian philosophers' proselytization parading itself under the guise of humility. The "brothers and sisters" who are ultimately the source of the eleven articles are informed by their own experiences doing the work of Christ in the world, having already committed large portions of their lives to the works which give life to faith — something that I hope comes across in reading the document.

---

8 Available in translation: John Howard Yoder, "Schleitheim Confession," accessed April 27, 2014, http://www.anabaptistwiki.org/mediawiki/index.php?title=Schleitheim_Confession_%28source%29.

9 Bonnie P. Lofton, "'Shenandoah Confession' Emerges from 2014 Intercollegiate Peace Meeting, in Spirit of 1527 Schleitheim Confession," *EMU News* (February 28, 2014).

10 Joel 2:28, NIV.

The universalism embedded in the Shenandoah Confession is inherent to the structure of the ideas of a universal Christ, and not some liberal ecumenical language of inclusion. A truly pacifist ethic must flow from a pacifist ontology, and this is one of the ongoing projects that my generation of thinkers has taken up.[11] Because of the theological background of its participants, the Shenandoah Confession speaks also to those in our generation inclined to identify as anarchists. The confession, I hope, can establish an understanding with a group of disaffected young brothers and sisters (like my friends at Occupy Charlottesville,) saying "no" to institutionalized authority, but saying "yes" to a natural form of authority — that form which I believe will ultimately reveal the servant nature of Christ, who inverted the authority of the world and whose yoke is easy.[12]

Speaking from my own experience (and not necessarily for the others who helped to draft the confession), the revolutionary potential of a work like the Shenandoah Confession is that it might speak to anarchists and veterans, LGBT crusaders and Marxists. The intention is not directly evangelistic, and this has been a turnoff to some on the Mennonite right; but the invitation of the Shenandoah Confession to participate in the suffering of the Lamb is radically conservative in a way that seeks to bring conservatives and radicals into conversation together. The truth of Jesus may be political truth, but it is freed from the false dualism imposed on our worldly politics by the powers and principalities.[13]

It was this relational truth — the plural, anexact and yet rigorous, timeless and universal truth of the Logos — that the Occupiers and the Anabaptists

---

11 *Co-Editors regret that this footnote was omitted from the print issue.*

I am thinking of young theologians like Nathan Hershberger, Thomas Millary, Jordan Luther, Andrea De Avila-Bilboa, Emily Hodges, and Jossimar Diaz-Castro, influenced in turn by thinkers like Peter Dula, Ted Grimsrud, J. H. Yoder, Peter Rollins, Jacques Ellul, and Slavoj Zizek.

12 *Co-Editors regret that this footnote was omitted from the print issue.*
Mark 10:44 and Matt. 11:30.

13 *Co-Editors regret that this footnote was omitted from the print issue.*

I am thinking of John Howard Yoder, The Politics of Jesus (Grand Rapids, MI: Eerdmans, 1972), and Walter Wink's The Powers trilogy (Philadelphia, PA: Fortress Press, 1984–86).

have been seeking in our separate communities.[14] It is long since time for the Mennonite community to come out of its shell and engage those thirsting for justice, and I pray that the Shenandoah Confession can be a first step in that process.

The Confession

Presented this 24th day of February, 2014, on behalf of those gathered in Christ at the Intercollegiate Peace Fellowship of Anabaptist colleges meeting at Eastern Mennonite University, to our various communities around the world. Written by participants with inspiration from previous Anabaptist confessions of faith.

Preface

May peace, fellowship, patience and the truth of the love of God be with all who love God. Beloved brothers and sisters in the Lord, may the care of the good shepherd and the strength of the lamb who was slain sustain you in your efforts to recognize God's Kingdom which, according to the most holy teacher and savior, Jesus of Nazareth, exists among and within all creation and is the source of life everywhere.

Dear brothers and sisters, we who have been assembled for the 2014 Intercollegiate Peace Fellowship Conference, in the Lord at Eastern Mennonite Seminary in the Shenandoah Valley of Virginia, make known to all that we have been united in the spirit of fellowship to the common goal of building the peace of a loving and merciful God. The articles to which we confess ourselves we announce here in the spirit of those Anabaptist brothers and sisters who before us made confession together at Schleitheim on the 24th day of February in the year 1527, and Dordrecht in 1632, including the various conclusions that have been amended to it by the church since. As those dear brothers and sisters made formal confession into a foundational action of the Anabaptist church, so let us confess ourselves in the hopes of a new and prophetic life in Immanuel, who is God with us.

---

14 *Co-Editors regret that this footnote was omitted from the print issue.*

This conception of theological truth builds on several sources. First and foremost is the philosophy of religion of Christian Early, heavily influenced by Nancey Murphey, Imre Lakatos, William Placher, and others. The term "anexact yet rigorous" is taken from the philosophy of science of Gilles Deleuze and Felix Guattari, explicated in their essay Nomadology: The War Machine (New York, NY: Semiotext(e), 1986). Essentially, I would argue, the theological truth and scientific truth are fully compatible in this system.

The eleven articles of confession

The articles of our confession are as follows:

1. Confession of faith in Christ as the foundation of peace.
2. Love as the root of all things.
3. The call of the spirit of God to all for radical pacifist action.
4. Acceptance of the truth of the full humanity of all God's children.
5. Inclusion as the guiding principle of action within the spirit.
6. Accountability of historical wrongs, especially colonialisms.
7. An abiding desire to participate in resilient and just economies.
8. The full and unflinching engagement of creative faculties of believers in service of peace.
9. Embrace of lives of radical simplicity following the truth of God's peace on Earth.
10. Commitment to deep listening and dialogue as the prophetic intention of Christian pacifism.
11. Recognition of failures and continued re-commitment to our principles within community.

Explication of articles

Confession of faith in Christ as the foundation of peace. We confess our faith in the peace of Christ that surpasses understanding, and our dedication to the principled peace of the Lord and savior Jesus who taught a bold humility. We embrace the faith even as we work for the good of all people, including people with whom we disagree, or people of other faiths, and even those who proclaim themselves our enemies and seek to do us harm. We seek the realization of the one we follow, Jesus, that the good of all is the work of servants; and in the tradition of him who laid down his life for all people, we embrace our identities as his followers knowing well the consequences of the burden of the cross. We admit that there can be no higher calling than the gospel call to nonviolent action in accordance with the will of the Holy Spirit, and the imminent fullness of the kingdom of the lamb, who does justice with mercy.

Love as the root of all things. Being created in the spirit of love, and saved by the love of Jesus who is our redeemed example of love, we here confess that love to be at the heart of all things. We confess to loving ourselves and others without the world's judgment and vanities; we commit to loving the earth and protecting God's gift of life, the spirit of God itself, and our enemies and neighbors, in praise and thanksgiving. We also confess our belief that our love must be one that challenges those around us to become better followers of Jesus. Love must be mission, holding others accountable and building them up. True love, we hold, calls people to action in its embodiment and by its very example.

The call of the spirit of God to all for radical pacifist action. This gospel call to act as servants we confess to be the central tenant of the Christian faith. Peace is the vocation of all things made by a just and good creator, we believe. Peace shapes our daily lives and actions whether or not we are aware of it; it is our intention to practice this peace conscientiously around the world and amongst neighbors. The spirit of God calls all God's life back to God, clothed in the raiment of nonviolence, worshiping the wonderful counselor who does justice and loves mercy. We confess that we seek to build institutions upon the shoulders of Christ, the servant who yearns for right relationship among the children of God.

Acceptance of the truth of the full humanity of all God's children. We affirm all brothers and sisters to be equal in Christ. We call for the full privileges and rights of Christ to be granted them without delay. We honor the power and beauty of all life, and seek to enter relationship with it, not avoiding but rather walking toward conflict in the spirit of peace and fellowship. Along with this, we confess that our communities must become places of deep healing, sustainable praxis, nonviolent education and radical acceptance, where brothers and sisters can seek their identities in Christ freely, without fear of prejudice or categorical pre-judgment.

Inclusion as the guiding principle of action within the spirit. We confess that the guiding principle of prophetic action within the will of the spirit is one of active inclusion. In Christ there is neither Jew nor Greek, slave nor free, nor male and female. All people, created in the image of God, are unconditionally welcomed to God's table and to God's salvation.

Accountability of historical wrong, especially colonialisms. We hereby pledge solidarity and yield up positions of leadership to those communities who have been historically marginalized. We seek to affirm their leadership and support peace and nonviolence education by upholding the principles of peacebuilding in our own local and historical contexts. As North American Anabaptists, we confess our need to challenge and reform our own government and lay out peacebuilding alternatives to violence and war.

An abiding desire to participate in resilient and just economies. We see that our world suffers from a lack of care for God's living environment, and we grieve the lack of our participation in an economy that is environmentally sustainable and socially just. We confess our desire to support local enterprise, invest prudently in clean energy, and remain mindful of our impact on and our role within God's loving creation. We seek to embrace trickle-up change, and we commit to imagining innovative communities along these principles near to our homes, even as we seek God's peace farther from our immediate spheres of influence.

The full and unflinching engagement of creative faculties of believers in service of peace. We confess that we look for creative engagement within our hearts and communities in order to nonviolently pursue restorative justice in the name of a righteous God of wholeness. Violence stifles creative impulses and inhibits our ability to seek the peace of God. We believe in appealing for peace to the creativity of the Spirit, which is that of Jesus, and of the one who sent him.

Embrace of lives of radical simplicity following the truth of God's peace on Earth. In order to focus our lives to the call of God's peace on Earth, we hereby uphold the life of the servant Christ in its simplicity and mission-orientation as the model for all conscientious human activity. We seek to affirm the intentional community of believers without excluding other brothers and sisters, and we disavow egotistical ambition as a basis for peace and faith work. We recognize the impossibility of following two masters, and choose to follow the way of peace despite the possibilities of worldly poverty which can sometimes overshadow it.

Commitment to deep listening and dialogue as the prophetic intention of Christian pacifism. We assert principles of right relationship to neighbor, enemy and self to be the following: deep listening as a means of connection and dialogue; openness to change of identity and opinion; mutual transformation in partnership and in the spirit of the creator; deep reflection before action; and nonviolence.

Recognition of failures and continued re-commitment to our principles within community. We confess that we have at times failed to embody the principles of community. With contrition we earnestly implore God's forgiveness. We have not loved our neighbors as ourselves, we have not honored God's creation, and we have often left the work of peace undone. Brothers and sisters in Christ, let us recognize our many vanities, our mindless consumerisms. Let us hereby recommit ourselves to the principles of Christian pacifism, the articles of confession above, and the teachings of Jesus of Nazareth in the way of nonviolence.

Postlude

Brothers and sisters in God, we most earnestly confess these points to you in hope that they move in your hearts, and excite within you a desire to confess them also. May your roots — watered in the innocence and strength of the lamb of God — nourish your spirits and give you rest and joy. Also may your wings — lifted by the breath of the Holy Spirit — shield you in the protection of the most high and allow you to walk and not grow faint, to run and not become weary, to soar as eagles. May the peace of God be with you now and always, and may the teachings of the Prince of Peace guide you to the realization of God's presence among us.

Amen.

Evangelicalism, Anabaptism, and Being the Church in a Post-Christian Culture:

An Interview with David Fitch

Carmen Andres[1]

Introduction

North American culture is undergoing a profound post-Christian shift. As a culture, we are moving away from shared language and assumptions of Christianity. The church as we've known it is moving to the margins.

As the broader North American church struggles with how to be the church in a culture that is growing increasingly disinterested in God and religion, there has been a growing interest in Anabaptism as a resource for addressing our cultural context. A growing number of Anabaptist voices are joining larger conversations taking place across theological traditions, particularly Evangelicalism.

Along the way, we've also seen the rise of Neo-Anabaptism, a term that still seems a bit fluid in definition. Some use it to refer to those who have come to Anabaptism from some other tradition and embrace it from or outside a traditional Anabaptist place. Others use it to describe those who seek to learn from Anabaptist history and incorporate the theology into other theologies or approaches. Still others emphasize it being influenced by post-modern and -colonial thought, particularly the critique of power. An approach to Anabaptism through the writings of Stanley Hauerwas and John Howard Yoder is yet another aspect I have encountered in relation to this term.

Last year, I attended the inaugural gathering of Missio Alliance, a collaborative movement among Evangelicals across a range of theological traditions who are seeking theological and practical guidance in facing what it means to be the church in an increasingly post-Christian culture. Interestingly, the conference enjoyed a solid presence of Anabaptist voices, ranging from those

---

1 *Carmen Andres is the former editor of the* Christian Leader, *the monthly magazine of the US Conference of Mennonite Brethren Churches. She writes a regular column for* Mennonite World Review *and currently works as a communications consultant in Northern Virginia, where she lives with her husband and two children.*

in historical Anabaptist traditions to those who identify themselves as Anabaptists within other theological bodies.

Dr. David Fitch was one of the latter. David, who defines himself as an evangelical Anabaptist, is an original founder and current board member of Missio Alliance. He is also the founding pastor of Life on the Vine Christian Community, a missional church in the northwest suburbs of Chicago, and the B. R. Lindner Chair of Evangelical Theology at Northern Seminary. With fellow Life on the Vine pastor, Geoff Holsclaw, David co-authored *Prodigal Christianity*, which explores and offers a creative vision for missional theology and practice in a post-Christian culture.

Recently, I reached out to David to talk with him about the ongoing and growing conversation between Evangelicalism and Anabaptism, Neo-Anabaptism, and what it means to be the church in a post-Christian world.

Interview

Carmen Andres*: If I'm not mistaken, you grew up outside of a denomination that stands in the Anabaptist tradition, yet found a home within its theological vision. Briefly, tell us about that journey. How did you come to find a home in Anabaptism?*

David Fitch: I grew up your classic white mainstream Evangelical. Then I came to the realization that mainstream Evangelicalism was not engaging the cultural issues that I was being faced with as someone in their twenties. Going off to seminary (I went to three or four different evangelical seminaries), I became disillusioned with evangelical fundamentalism. I went to a more classic liberal seminary, Garrett Evangelical, and did my PhD at Northwestern University. I found Protestant liberalism to be a different version of the same and equally as vacuous as evangelical fundamentalism. It accommodated cultural issues; it didn't engage them.

So, to make a long story short, it was really through that prolonged intellectual struggle in my life — which also entailed working as a financial services account executive for a while, so I was in the world, so to speak — that I arrived at Stanley Hauerwas. He reset or disrupted the existing categories completely and gave me the wherewithal to navigate a world that had completely and totally shifted in my lifetime. That journey then led me to John Howard Yoder (RYFC).

CA*: Why did you include "RYFC" after Yoder?*

DF: Whenever I quote Yoder now I put in parenthesis "RYFC," an acrostic for "recognizing Yoder's flawed character." It's important that my Mennonite USA brothers and sisters know that I am aware that there are some difficulties here.

Having said that, those figures — Hauerwas, Yoder, and then there came philosophical figures like Charles Taylor, Steven Toulmin, and Alastair MacIntyre back in the early 1990s — helped me piece together a way of being Christian authentically in the world. From there on, I became a leader in churches, organizing communities of mission, and got involved in the missional church movement with some of my early writings. And I just got deeper and deeper and thicker and thicker into the leading question of the church's engagement with the surrounding culture. And, to be honest with you, the Anabaptist and the Neo-Anabaptist frameworks were the ones that helped me the most.

CA*: You mentioned Neo-Anabaptism. Is Neo-Anabaptist a term you use to describe yourself?*

DF: Yes.

CA*: How do you define the term?*

DF: I use Neo-Anabaptist to differentiate myself from historical Anabaptists. And yet, I am jumping onto themes that have been sustained within the Anabaptist movements — and I say "movements" in the plural because, in my experience, there is no one pure stream of Anabaptist thought, at least historically.

For example, we have these themes about post-Christendom, or Constantinianism. We examine the church's relationship to the state and all power structures; we question alliance with them as protocol. Once you take that out of the picture — that the church is no longer aligned with the state and power structures in society — discipleship becomes really important because we can't depend on the state to keep us in line or to guide us in our life. We as his people must ourselves be responsible to follow Jesus. So, the Person and work of Jesus and Christology take the center place in our life.

And of course kingdom becomes really important as opposed to an individualistic kind of Protestant spirituality. This becomes a whole life discipleship under the lordship of Christ. And that means there's going to be a community that's at the center of our lives, and that's going to be the church. The hermeneutic of the community is going to take a central place in our lives because we're not depending on the broad culture anymore to tell us what to do.

And then lastly, out of all this comes the understanding of nonviolence and peace — that God has not chosen to enter into the world and redeem the world through violence, through coercion, or through hierarchy, but he comes in and through relationship, reconciliation, peace, renewal by the cross and the resurrection. Those are all immensely important Anabaptist themes, and they really come out of a different way of self-understanding that happened within the first Anabaptists, who saw that they really couldn't become aligned with various state forms of Christianity in Europe in the fifteenth and sixteenth centuries.

So, that's the Anabaptist part. But then there is the "neo" part of it — and it all depends on who you're dealing with. But we're all working off post-Enlightenment, post-liberal, or post-structuralist ways of thought. Some call it postmodern ways of thought: this loss of foundations in society, the loss of hegemony by one culture. I personally play off of the radical democracy movement, political theorists like Slavoj Zizek, ideological cynicism, how we understand the formation of ideologies, and how it takes a community to even engage and not be thrust into the power of ideologies that shape us.

And so "neo" means we're working off of all those ways of thought. We could include Hauerwas as the founder, but Hauerwas was playing off Yoder, the Yale school, postmodern hermeneutics, Wittgenstein — all those things. That's the "neo" part of it; the old themes with the current philosophical constructs that we're all trying to figure out, and they just fit together like hand and glove — for me, anyways.

CA: In addition to Neo-Anabaptist you've also used the word "missional" a couple of times. We hear that word tossed around a lot these days. How do you define missional? In what ways did Anabaptism help you shape the way you approach or define it?

DF: First, the missional movement has emerged or been birthed in both Protestant mainline and evangelical churches. Some common themes are that God is at work in the world, that God — in the sending of his Son and the professing of his Spirit into the world — is a *sending* God, and that God has a mission and that's part of who he is. And the church is part of that mission. It's not the church that has a mission, but it's *God* that has a mission and the church is part of it. The church is part of something bigger than itself, and so the church must be engaged outside its four walls to be truly authentic in its life with God in mission.

The second piece or realization of the missional movement is that God has come in Christ incarnationally to be with and among us. That means we too have to be with and among people. We can't segregate ourselves off into a bunch of attractional services that ask people to come to us, get what they need, and then go home and live in isolation.

At first glance, you might think some of those themes are in antagonism with Anabaptism, but I would argue, no. When we see that we are in a post-Christendom world and we're no longer a massive Protestant consensus of the United States of America, we can see that we're actually in mission. That helps us understand the new dynamics of the church.

We have a lot learn from the Anabaptist movements in terms of how we engage a world as a minority — because we *are* now a minority. We're not a majority, and we're not in power anymore — just like the Anabaptists said we always should be, we now are, and now we have to deal with it. The Anabaptists have already been dealing with it, and they can help us think through it again.

Likewise, with incarnation. The Anabaptists teach us how to be local and engaged on our own terms — humbly, nonviolently, in service *to* our local community. We do this not by taking into our own hands the power of a state or a broad universalist logic — whatever you use to impose your will on society. No, we must be local and engaged communities of witness. That's one of the strengths of the Anabaptist thought.

So, when you put these things together — post-Christendom, discipleship, nonviolence, community, local community engagement — that's a whole way of engaging the world that helps missional people. A lot of us come from Protestant mainline denominations who are used to being in power, or we are even Evangelicals who still think we are in power, and we don't know how to think in the Anabaptist way. We need to learn from the Anabaptists.

CA: You've talked a little about how you have been formed by historic Anabaptist thinkers and writers. Have you had interactions with historic Anabaptist communities? What do you see as their current role in the theological discourse?

DF: I'm an evangelical Anabaptist. That probably makes no sense to many of my Mennonite brothers and sisters because when they hear the word evangelical they think George W. Bush or Republican politics. Predominant in Evangelicalism is either Jerry Farwell or Jim Wallis, both of whom (even though Wallis originally, I think, had Anabaptist impulses in his thought) have become people who want to align the transformation of society with state politics.

Well, that's not all of us Evangelicals. I'm an Evangelical who sees the main impetuses of Evangelicalism as being a respect for the authority and the history of Scripture, the centrality of the cross, and the Person and the work of Jesus Christ and the supremacy of that work. We also have an evangelical activism about us that, at certain social times in our history, has been mainly, "Let's get the gospel out to as many people as we can." I think those impulses are helpful for the Anabaptist world to listen to and hear from, but also we Evangelicals need to reframe those strengths with the humility and the insights of true Anabaptist thought.

I think that the conversation between the Evangelicals and Anabaptists is immensely important. Every time I go speak with Mennonite and Anabaptist groups or I'm invited onto their campuses to talk, I learn something that reshapes how I think about the practice of church and the practice of evangelism. Likewise, I think that I've been able to be an encouragement to Anabaptist groups in the way I say, "Hey, you already have within your traditions many of the worked-out historical solutions — or at least directions to go — to deal with the cultural dilemmas all of us Christians are facing in the new post-Christendom West, in North America and Europe."

I'll give you one more example. Some parts of the Mennonite world have been active in peacemaking and that trail blazed for all of us how to work for peace and not just talk about peace, not just talk about a kind of withdrawal pacifism. No, let's be out there being witnesses to, cooperating with, and working for the peace of Christ.

Evangelicals can learn from Mennonites and Anabaptists, and Anabaptists can learn from us. We can learn from John Howard Yoder (RYFC), and we can learn that to say "Jesus is Lord" is to also say "we are not." And therefore we can enter in with humility, vulnerability, and mutual submission, and submit to what God's doing in the conflicts with other religions, the conflicts between tribes, and the conflicts between nation states. We can bring peace, and we don't have to deny the supremacy of Christ. I think that's where Evangelicals and Mennonites and Anabaptists can learn from each other.

I hope that's helpful. I'm talking with a lot of nuances.

CA: *Having lived and worshiped in Mennonite Brethren churches, I appreciate your observations on the tensions between Evangelicalism and Anabaptism and ways we can learn from each other. You've mentioned the nonviolence or peacemaking aspect of Anabaptism. How does peacemaking impact your life and the way that you live?*

DF: It takes all the coercion and the anxiety out of evangelism. We Evangelicals believe in evangelism, but often we've been unaware of the power posture that we take in the world. For a long while we were in charge, or at least we thought we were — and some of us still think we are. We're not, but some people still think we are.

So, what Anabaptism helps us understand is that we are no longer in charge. God is in charge, and God is at work. Evangelism becomes a posture of being present *with* the least of these, the hurting, all people and being patient. We just let God do what he is going to do through our witness so that when someone comes up to us and says, "What is this thing that makes you tick?" we're always there ready to give an account, as 1 Peter says, of the hope that is within us.

It takes the coercion out. When we engage our culture, we no longer engage it out of a posture of power — we know what's best for you, we know what you need to do with your schools, we know what you need to do with your hospitals, we know what you need to do with this, this, and this problem. No, it enters a place quietly *in submission* as servants and quietly discerns what's going on with God in our midst and around us. And one by one, we give witness to what God is doing in evangelistic efforts and in social justice efforts, just by being present and patient.

Those are themes — humility, incarnation, nonviolence — that Anabaptists can teach us a lot about how to inhabit as a way of life. We now become convinced that God does not work in the world through violence, through coercion. That's not the way he works. There will be no salvation, there will be no redemption, there will be no renewing of all things through those things. There might be preservation of some things, but there will not be renewal or redemption of all things through any of that.

So that's how we live our lives and that informs so much of life on the ground in mission. It changes, I would argue, the whole ballgame.

CA*: You've talked about how Anabaptism is speaking into and helping us understand the increasingly post-Christian cultural context that we're living in, especially the valuable insights Anabaptists bring to the conversation because of their experience of being on the margins. Missio Alliance is sponsoring a conference this September to explore the way Anabaptist thought and theology is a growing resource for shaping missional approaches and witness in this cultural context and provides some answers to a growing weariness of polarities in evangelicalism. I would argue that there is a growing weariness with polarities even within the historical Anabaptist churches as well. Can you talk about this some more?*

DF: I agree with you that, in my small interactions within Anabaptist traditions, their schools and churches, there is a wearisomeness with the internal battles and polarities just like there is in Evangelicalism.

Let me give you an insight into what's going on in the life and thought of the Neo-Anabaptist movement. We're seeing two extreme reactions — and this is even true in missional thought. First is a defensive reaction. "The Bible says this" or "You need to get in line" are responses of a withdrawal from or failure to communicate across lines in the culture. On the other hand, there's accommodation — "We agree with you," "We want to support you with whatever you're doing," and "God is at work in everything you're doing, let us affirm you, come alongside of you" are common phrases we hear. In both cases we lose mission because either we withdraw and get defensive and antagonistic against culture, or we totally inhabit and bring nothing to culture.

Anabaptism refuses those frameworks. It almost overcomes and throws them upside-down. Let me fill in what I mean by upside-down. We don't even see that by inhabiting a community of the kingdom we're not making judgments against or for the culture. We are now *in* and *with* the culture, discerning what God's doing. And we are no longer in control. Both the accommodative and the defensive positions want to maintain control and stay in power. When you give up power, you lose a lot of the problems.

So, Anabaptist thought and vision is speaking into the cultural challenges that we're facing in ways that these two traditions — Evangelicalism and Protestant mainline thought as well as, I think, the Anabaptists themselves — need to come to grips with and find refreshing. And I think that's where a lot of the attention and enthusiasm is coming from and why this conference is even going to take place. There's just a lot of interest. People are asking, "Please help us find a way out of this antagonistic mess we're in. It sure looks like you're saying some fresh things that seem to make a lot of sense." So, there are resources here for evangelicals.

CA: *You also speak about this weariness and discontent a growing number of us in North America are experiencing with theological and political labels and polarities in* Prodigal Christianity, *a book you wrote with Geoff Holsclaw, with whom you pastored Life on the Vine for ten years. Tell us a little about the book and why you and Geoff wrote it.*

DF: The book's about how to reframe being church in the world, locally engaged, incarnationally — and what are the theological frameworks for that, and how do we think about gospel, Scripture, and church as a result of those frameworks.

For me, the most engaging part of the book is how this changes the way we frame the cultural challenges of our day. In the book, we address three of them: the world of injustice and political powers, the world of alternative sexualities, and the world of pluralist religions. How do we live our lives as witness to the kingdom of God in the midst of these three things? Those three areas are dividing our churches or, at least, they are dividing our evangelical churches. I think they might be dividing a lot of Anabaptist driven churches as well.

I wanted to show how, by making a space for the practice of the kingdom, these things get worked out in transformative ways — largely via noncoercive, nonviolent practices. Out of mutual submission to the lordship of Christ, the gifts of the Holy Spirit, the basic core practices of being the people of God, and his presence in the world, God starts to work and God transforms. It's a whole new way of engaging our world as the church.

Now when I say a whole new way, I'm an Anabaptist; I don't think it's new at all. I think it was the way things were for a couple hundred years before the Constantinian synthesis happened. We've been trying to rid ourselves of some of those bad habits for a long time. So, it's just reconstituting some of the ways of being the church — you might say John Howard Yoder's body practices (RYFC) translated and put into practical use for a missional local congregation.

CA: *You've mentioned several times this theme of noncoercive and nonviolent practices in place of power and control. As I was reading your book, I was attracted to the model you present and yet at the same time I was thinking this is a scary way to go because you are giving up control and power.*

DF: It's a never ending battle. We want to take control. We work for justice — but for *your* justice and *your* views of justice. You want control. But it's not about you, and it's not about *your* justice. God's at work bringing *his* justice in through Jesus Christ. Can you cooperate?

The minute you overstep the boundaries of violence, coercion, hierarchy, patriarchy — all the things that humans use to control — God's power and his ability to work in a situation is removed. *He* removes it; he will not cooperate with the violence of the world. That's a little oversimplified, but I think you get what I'm saying. God can use violence in ulterior ways but, ultimately, that's not his direct way of overcoming evil in the world.

CA: *Do you see this concept of power and the way God prefers a nonviolent way of working as distinctly Anabaptist?*

DF: I'm almost prepared to say an unqualified yes. That's the insight of Anabaptists. The insight is implicit, if not explicit, throughout the Anabaptist processes. Even Münster, when they made the huge mistakes, out of that we learn violence is a mistake. So, it's implicit everywhere in the Anabaptist movement, but it becomes most prominent and best systemized through the 1960s, 70s, and 80s and the work of John Howard Yoder (RYFC).

CA: *A criticism of Anabaptists in North America is that some areas of leadership are made up largely of middle class white men, and the lack of people of color and women's voices is a sad fact when it comes to some theological and church conversations. How can an Anabaptist identity shape our response to this problem? What can we do to bring these voices to the conversation?*

DF: First of all, I believe Anabaptism and Neo-Anabaptism have the best singular response to power and hierarchy. If women are not full participants in the ministry of the church, it's a denial of who we are as Anabaptists.

If there's anyone who should be able to overcome patriarchy, it should be Anabaptists; therefore we are not being true to ourselves if we have not extolled women in the ministry. It's in our theology. I can't speak for Anabaptist history — I don't understand it all — but I know that Evangelicalism got co-opted by power and certain logics having to do with Scripture. That's where we lost it. I don't know how Anabaptists lost it, but we must recover it. And we are recovering it, big time.

Let me add this: anytime women have been in ministry with the charismatic gifts of the Holy Spirit in full authority with men, the church has exploded. Anytime women have been out of authority due to patriarchy or hierarchy, the church has turned into a maintenance organization. We have to understand that, and we need to understand that Anabaptist thought is one of the best contributors for women empowered for full authority there is in the Christian history.

On the racial diversity issue, Anabaptism comes from Europe; it's historically white. Sometimes it takes white men speaking to white men, or white people speaking to white people, to call them into who they are. Sometimes, that's the way it's going to look. We've got to tell ourselves what's wrong with us ourselves, and it's already there in our history to do that. We need to call ourselves to righteousness.

In the same way, there is a logic in Anabaptist thought that is so powerful and so central to racial reconciliation, and therefore we should be at the forefront of this.

Both Evangelicals and Protestant mainline churches are on course with diversity, racial reconciliation and a reflection of the church as Jew–Gentile, as one. But the problem is that we subsume our efforts to implementations of power relationships which have more to do with enforcement as opposed to the practice — the very core practice of reconciliation and presence one with another.

I hope you got what I'm trying to say there. What happens is we either do something mechanically where we have the token African American in a conference — which no one, including the African American, buys — or we try to manufacture diversity through various means. I am, by the way, an admirer of affirmative action, and I think quotas sometimes have to take place. I support laws and civil rights. But these efforts are basically going to be preservatory. They're going to preserve and order something which is still mechanical.

It's not until we actually become *present* with one another, live alongside one another, get to know one another, hear our stories — not so that cultures are obliterated but where all differences are respected yet all are mutually submitted to — that a new thing is birthed that no one can manufacture. It's a work of God.

For that to happen, it has to be grass roots, on the ground — and there's nobody better prepared to do that or who understands those dynamics better than, in my opinion, the Anabaptists. Granted, we have failed at this in many ways, but it's there and it's ready to go.

Read James Cone's book, *Martin & Malcolm & America*. Martin Luther King tried to integrate Blacks with the white dominant culture and, in his later opinion, the Black person in America got subsumed into power relationships with white people. It didn't work. Likewise, Malcolm X said the Black race has to have an integrity unto its own self; he said until we have integrity ourselves we cannot relate to anybody else. And he was right on that. But he believed the only way to do that was violence; he was wrong on that one. One place where the best of Martin Luther King and the best of Malcolm X's theologies come together is in Anabaptist thought.

CA: *What do you mean that the best of both come together in true Anabaptist thought?*

DF: According to James Cone, the early Martin Luther King understood nonviolence, but he subsumed the Black concerns into white ones. He integrated Blacks into existing white society not understanding that white society was polluted with corrupt power relationships. This was Malcolm X's critique of MLK. On the other hand, Malcolm X understood the need for an inherent identity or else the Black American would get obliterated by the white dominant culture, but he didn't understand nonviolence like Martin Luther King.

Anabaptist thought, in my opinion, brings the nonviolence of Martin Luther King and the integrity of each culture of Malcolm X, including the African American, together in one mutual submission space with all races, and God creates a new thing. The practices of mutual submission, nonviolence, communal hermeneutics, local engaged practices of Eucharist, reconciliation of being with one another — those are the places where that can happen. And the Anabaptists should be at the forefront of that. We have to be the ones at the forefront of God working a new diverse people of one Lord and one baptism. To me the Christian Community Development Association movement as led by John Perkins is a place we Anabaptist types can go to learn what our own theology looks like on the ground in terms of bringing racial reconciliation and renewal to our neighborhoods.

CA: *We've talked a lot about our North American experiences. Have you had conversations with those outside North America about the challenges we are facing here* *regarding post-Christian culture? Who are the voices that we need to be listening to outside of North America that can help us as navigate this new terrain for us?*

DF: I grew up in Canada, and I'm well familiar with the cultural issues in churches there. And I've spent some significant time in France working with international workers. My evangelical circles are just awakening to what Anabaptist theology is. Yet each time I talk or present, bells go off, light bulbs turn on, and a whole new way of understanding mission is enabled by the categories of Anabaptist theology, practice, and church.

Emmanuel Katongole wrote a book called *The Sacrifice of Africa*. I can't really say it's Anabaptist but, my goodness, if anything unwinds the colonialist problems that remain in Africa after the colonialist regimes have left and discusses overcoming the recycling of colonialist power structures in developing world countries like those in Africa, that's the book. As an African and a Roman Catholic priest, he gets the issues of power and working for peace. His book would be at the top of my list of voices and places where people are working on the ground for the peaceful formation of communities of mission and peace to overcome violence.

CA: *One last question. For all of the talk about the shift in global Christianity from North to South, significant power — particularly economic — differentials remain, leaving the impression among many that this new global reality is simply an old case of "separate but equal." Given that, what actually connects or fosters relationships between North and South that reflects the biblical image of the body of Christ? What does Anabaptist thought have to teach us about this?*

DF: For years the United States has looked at the Global South in terms of the "haves" and the "have nots." We, the USA, are the "haves" and they are the "have nots." We have viewed these inequities in terms of Gross Domestic Product and other economic measurements based in capitalism. The Christian response was to push for aid in one direction, from those who have much to those who have much, much less. In all of this, we overlooked how our "help" in terms of money and resources exacerbated the power relationships that had caused the poverty and abuse in the first place. Many of those corrupt power regimes we must go through to distribute mass amounts of aid are the legacy of colonialist exploitation of the past from the West. We must break down how we indeed participate in these power relationships when we fund aid through them.

Neo-Anabaptist thought helps us see there is a lot more to the reordering of economic relationships than money. Capitalism is not the world's answer. It helps us see how we must in essence divest of power if we are to enter a place as a participant in renewal. If we seek to engage the world with our wealth, we must enter into space and time relationships where we are receivers as much as we are givers. Where we learn as much as we receive. Where our money becomes part of a reciprocity. Where we are purged of our own ills as much as we help and relieve those we inhabit the world with on the other side of the globe. This kind of mission is made uniquely possible by Neo-Anabaptist thought because it gives us a critique of capitalism, wealth, and American consumerism that enables us to be stripped of the illusion that our economic system is somehow good and will solve the world's problems.

CA: *Is there anything you'd like to add that we haven't talked about or that came up as we were talking?*

DF: It's time for Evangelicals to listen to Anabaptists. And if Anabaptists can give us grace for all our mistakes over the past hundred years, I think it would help Anabaptists to listen to us Evangelicals. But we need to come together in humility. Sometimes Evangelicals are not practiced in that, so Anabaptists probably need to give Evangelicals a little grace and patience. Having said that, I think it's a really important discussion to have.

Dignity in Cross-Cultural Relationships:

An Anabaptist Approach to Short-Term Missions

ROBERT THIESSEN[1]

Jesus' encounter with the Samaritan woman in Sychar, told in the fourth chapter of John, has ramifications for many areas of ministry. In this article I will examine the many ways this story can help us shape what we often call "short-term missions." Jesus' life and teachings serve for Anabaptists as the prism through which we view all Scripture, and how Jesus approaches this particular "short term" ministry is key.[2]

Jesus arrives at midday in the Samaritan lady's town after walking for hours with his disciples. While they go into town to find food, Jesus sits down to wait beside the well — one supposedly dug by Jacob over a millennium before. He is hungry, tired, and thirsty. Along comes a woman, alone, and (we assume) outcast, to draw water. Jesus, needing her help, asks for water. Something begins to take place that moves this woman to share her discovery of living water with the very townspeople who had ostracized her.

This story, at its heart, is about human dignity. Over and over Jesus shows how much he values and dignifies individuals, but never more than here. From the outset we notice Jesus' condition — he is decidedly in a position of need, and with nothing to offer. He is "the very likeness of God," and yet he cannot even get a pot of water for himself! He is alone (at least for this moment) and starts the conversation by asking the woman for something she can give. How different from the way many short-term missionaries operate!

Although we know little about this woman's life, we can make some guess-

---

1 *Written January 2014 by Robert Thiessen of southern Ontario, Canada. Robert lives with his wife, Anne, and two children (Ruth and Philip), among Mixtec indigenous people in the states of Guerrero and Oaxaca, Mexico. He serves with MBMission, Abbotsford, BC, Canada (North American Mennonite Brethren Church), and is also associated with Moravians in North Carolina, and the Unity of the Brethren in Texas.*

2 Jacob Loewen: "[R]adical reformers insisted on a 'focused' view of the canon . . . a powerful exegetical principle. It defined not only the core value of Scripture — Jesus' life and teaching — but by giving equal rank to teaching and life it postulated that word and deed are inseparable dimensions of faith. Furthermore, Jesus' teaching and life functioned as a prism through which all scriptural truth was to be filtered for interpretation." Jacob Loewen, *Only the Sword of the Spirit* (Kindred Productions, 1997), 207.

es, since she arrives at midday without female companions, and she has "had five husbands." I have asked dozens of groups to act this story out, and inevitably, probably because of this detail, they choose a young "sexy" girl to play her part. They think of her as something akin to a prostitute. But after living twenty years among a marginalized indigenous group in southern Mexico, I see this woman differently. Now I imagine her as one of the Mixtec women I have known — married off by an emotionally distant father at thirteen, abandoned by her husband after having two children, and now taking up with new partners who can put corn in the pot. With each new partner (and child), she becomes less marriageable. She might be only thirty-five, but she looks worn and used up, aged far beyond her years. Other women around her, lucky enough to miss a similar story, shun her as a threat to their own marriages, a bearer of bad karma. She has lived a "hell on earth," sinking deeper into despair at each turn of the wheel.

The woman is unexpectedly asked by this Jewish rabbi to give him water, and begins to get a hint that her world is going to be turned on its head. Initially this is so out of her experience that she becomes defensive. After all, who has ever treated her with respect? She barely knows what that means. As the encounter unfolds, Jesus touches on her marriage situation, and she, adept at wiggling away from uncomfortable issues, asks a question she hopes will focus his attention elsewhere, a theological question that gets to the heart of the divide between Jew and Samaritan.

Jesus' answer is so powerful that to this day many people memorize these few verses (21–4) but remain ignorant of the overall context. He says (my paraphrase), "It doesn't matter where you've come from, what ethnic background; now is the time to worship God in spirit and in truth, in ways that no longer divide, but unite." This is even more shattering when we consider Jesus' purpose in life. Paul calls this purpose "the secret and mystery of the ages," and Jesus elsewhere says "that prophets longed to understand this" (Eph. 3:3–6,9 and Matt. 13:17). This mystery is what drives all missions, but especially short-term missions because they are often first-time encounters.

With his answer, Jesus shifts the woman's question into a different plane altogether, rising above argument to reach dialogue. Vincent Donovan, an iconoclastic Catholic missionary who served among the Masai in the 1970s, in a book that influenced many, describes it: "[D]o not try to call them back to where they were, [or] to where you are, as beautiful as that place might seem to you. You must have the courage to go with them to a place that neither you nor they have ever been before."[3] This encounter is the foundation of the church where differences between Jew and Gentile, male and female, rich and poor, sinner and righteous are undone, and where freedom and grace are realized.

The Samaritan woman is transformed. She leaps from the depths of her despair and begins to run, shouting all the way to those who despise her, that here, finally, is the Prophet, the one who brings life at the very point where she had felt most damned. The story later repeats what she says, "Come see this man who knows everything I've ever done. He knows who I am!" Her self-worth is restored, or maybe even just birthed. Jesus doesn't even mention the word "repent" (his first words in other Gospel accounts), but we know that repentance has come, because this is the birth of the first non-Jewish community of Christ followers (John 4:41–2).

The humble position of Jesus as a supplicant before the woman, and his expectation that she was prepared to respond to truth, sets the stage for all of this. Jesus, our guide to all truth, reveals what should be our own attitude. Paul defines it a bit more clearly, commanding us to have such a mind in Philippians 2: "Though [Jesus] was God, he did not think of equality with God as something to cling to. Instead, he gave up his divine privileges; he took the humble position of a slave and was born as a human being. When he appeared in human form, he humbled himself in obedience to God" (NLT). This should be the primary dynamic of all cross-cultural encounters of any time duration, whether days, weeks, years, or decades. So, what might that look like?

My wife and I have served in partnership with a variety of Anabaptist-affiliated agencies, congregations, and individuals over the years. Through these relationships, our team has organized and led perhaps several hundred people through short-term learning experiences over the last two decades. However, in my first years on the field, I avoided hosting short-term mission trips because everything I saw seemed to be premised on this assumption: "We have it together and want to share with you folks who are so needy. Here, let me show you how it's done. Let me fix this." I think that our Mennonite background makes us especially susceptible to this attitude (I was raised to practice farming and fix things, to be hardworking and handy with tools). However helpful our skills are, they don't always help us value people at the bottom of the social scale (of human making). Traditional Mennonite values of humility and modesty, which align so well with Paul's admonition in Philippians, seem to recede quickly when we meet people who may appear less practical or punctual, or analytical, or hardworking.

---

3 Vincent Donovan, *Christianity Today* (Orbis, 1993), vii.

After some time, though, I realized that my Hispanic friends gained something in such encounters: they built relationship with others in the kingdom, they shared their journeys, and they inspired one another. I had learned as a Mennonite to value community and discipleship, and this made me wonder if short-term trips could build relationships based on humility and respect while avoiding the pitfalls. Living among the indigenous Mixtec people while in Mexico, I learned over time how they longed for *to'o*, respect. This is perhaps their biggest "felt need"; they bemoaned lack of respect continually. Often, their encounters with outsiders degraded dignity, reinforcing their position at the bottom of the social scale. What better way to demonstrate respect than to have the travelers stay with my Mexican friends, enjoy their famous hospitality, and sleep in their beds, or on their floors, and eat their *chile*-laced food? So we began to offer this alternative to the traditional short-term trip, which has resulted in many beautiful cross-cultural relationships.

Now our church planting team in Mexico helps new members and short-term visitors focus on receiving and learning. The host families are the experts in their world, and the visitors are the tiny babes, often unable to even go to the restroom correctly. If short-termers can break out of their cultural bubble and go one by one to stay with host families, learning a few phrases of the local language daily, limiting themselves to the food served at locally normal hours, and observing another way of life while reserving judgment, then we honor people often dismissed by outsiders. If we can hold off on giving them our old clothes, building their buildings, preaching their sermons, or running their evangelistic campaigns, then we do what Jesus did when he first approached a new culture. There will be room to do more later on, but first we hope they will respond openly as the Samaritan woman did because we have valued them, respecting them as we would our own kind, and expecting that God has already been at work long before we arrived. If, through us, they experience Christ's acceptance — his valuing of what they already know and do — we gain the opportunity to share his news as good news, and when they share this message on their own as the Samaritan woman did, others are transformed as well. I believe that we too are transformed through this experience, and that together, two cultures walking hand-in-hand, we can be blessed as "God has come to dwell among us."

Anabaptists, especially those who struggle with contradictory North American values, should look to Jesus' practice and teachings to shape cross-cultural interaction. God's incarnation among us is itself critical to the kingdom of heaven, and of first importance as we forge relationships filled with hope and dignity with people from other cultures.

A Reopened Ending:

John 4:1–42 and the Church's Mission

DAVID DRIEDGER[1]

This sermon was presented at First Mennonite Church of Winnipeg on February 2, 2014. Reverend David Driedger here argues that the logic of colonialism remains a deeply embedded feature of Western Christian theology. Mennonites have at times been blind to this logic because we have focused on our own hardships, while neglecting the way this reasoning has been used by larger colonial forces. After identifying the logic of colonialism within John 4, Driedger here calls for the church to take on a posture of decolonialism, suggesting how we might reopen this biblical story in a way that might correct past abuses of mission.

Encountering the Logic of Colonialism

In preparation for sermons, I will sometimes search an academic database for relevant articles commenting on a given passage. Many times there are just a handful of papers, usually written by keen scholars pursuing some sort of historical accuracy or theological insight, many just plodding along with some sense of there being a "truth" to discover in Scripture.

However, when I searched the databases for commentary on John 4, I unexpectedly found a flourish of articles from a diverse range of scholars addressing many different issues related to the text. There were writers from North and South America, Europe, Africa, and India dealing with topics of mission, history, art, politics, gender, sociology, and philosophy. It is not uncommon to have a range of engagements with a biblical text, but these search results were so striking that it made me pause. Something significant is happening in this text. Up until chapter 4, John definitely made some grand claims, but these claims were made *within* the local Jewish context — this was a Jewish conversation.

Jesus crosses significant boundaries in John 4, including cultural, geographical, gender, and religious. We read in this chapter an early account of Christian mission. The typical reading of Jesus's encounter with the woman at

---

1 *David Driedger is Associate Minister at First Mennonite Church in Winnipeg, Manitoba.*

the well is one in which Jesus is portrayed as connecting with an outcast and marginal individual, offering her hope and acceptance. But, as I hope to explore here, the goodness of such an act may only be apparent within a certain logic.

This logic can take on many forms — in situations where there is a real sense or belief that what is being offered is good, right, and charitable. It might unfold in the story of a male professor providing sensitive encouragement to a young female grad student. It might be witnessed in an agricultural corporation selling their patented seeds to struggling rural areas in India. It is present in a Western military campaign bringing some version of democratic and economic structures to indigenous communities or Middle Eastern countries. It could be a religious leader or family member promising release from homosexual orientation. As good as these intentions might be, most of us have seen or experienced this logic as inappropriate or even damaging.

This logic is identified in many expressions of colonialism. 'Colonialism' commonly refers to how nations and groups have somehow occupied and controlled other nations or groups. The term comes from the European expansion of colonies beginning around the 15th century. The basic practice of conquering and controlling populations, however, is of course much older in the rise and fall of past empires.

Reading the Bible for Decolonization

In a troubling commentary on John 4, Musa Dube explores the relationship of the Bible to the European project of colonial expansion. She begins by quoting a well-known African saying, "When the white man came to our country he had the Bible and we had the land. The white man said to us, 'let us pray.' After the prayer, the white man had the land and we had the Bible."[2]

And so the history of Western Christian expansion unfolded within expressions of missionary zeal, economic and political aspirations, and conviction of theological superiority. With this history looming large and real in her homeland of Botswana, Dube addresses John 4, beginning with the larger context of the book itself. As is commonly accepted, it seems John was written later than the other Gospels and reflects the theology of a particular Christian Jewish community in which the book is believed to have been developed. One of the main features of this community is the tension they experienced within the synagogue and with other Jews. Through this Gospel there are indications of how volatile and divisive this tension was with many of the Christian Jews apparently being kicked out. Dube believes that this explains why the commu-

---

2 Musa Dube, "Reading for De-colonization (John 4:1-42)," *Semeia* 75 (1996): 37–59.

nity that shaped John's Gospel would have wanted to emphasize and forge a new alliance with the Samaritans.[3] As a marginal people themselves, Christian Jews were looking to shore up support and strength, even if it meant reaching out to Samaritans, who were generally considered "half-breeds", bastards essentially, by many Jews. New enemies can make friends of old enemies. And all these local politics are set within the larger setting of Roman rule and the need to consolidate as much support as possible.

Rather than joining the Pharisaic Jews or submitting fully to Roman rule, Christian Jews seem to construct their own colonial project. They claimed themselves as the ones expanding their kingdom, though surely they are doing it with good intentions. They are the ones doing it right? But this is where things get difficult. As I mentioned earlier, nearly every expression that *ends* with control or domination *began* with a sense of benevolence, a belief that something good was being offered. It is no different in John 4.

Jesus is portrayed as superior — he comes with special access to *living water.* Jesus plays on the woman's ignorance and perhaps even gender imbalance, telling her that she worships what she does not know, while Jesus, a Jew, possesses the true knowledge of salvation. What Jesus appeals to is abstract — the spirit of truth, something that is greater than her particular tradition, which is limited and insufficient. Jesus is constructing a notion of truth that can undermine and absorb any competing expression.

When the disciples return, Jesus tells them about their commissioning; their being sent out into the mission field which is ripe for the picking. Jesus says, "I have sent you to reap that for which you did not labor." How would an indigenous community hear that after experiences with Western expansion? They are passive fields just waiting to be cut down, presumably for the profit of salvation. *Now we have the Bible and they have the land.*

Finally, after hearing the words of the woman, the men of Samaria come out and affirm their allegiance to Jesus. They proclaim, discarding the woman's authority and affirming theirs, that Jesus "is truly the Savior of the world." This statement, "savior of the world," is a clear reference to Roman emperors.[4] Jesus is commander and chief of a rival nation and the Samaritans are aligning themselves with him. This reading of John 4 remains foreign to the majority interpretation of this text, but the history of the church's mission in the West demands that we consider this unsettling interpretation seriously.

---

3 Ibid., 47.

4 Wes Howard-Brook, *Becoming Children of God: John's Gospel and Radical Discipleship* (Eugene, OR: Wipf & Stock, 2003), 113.

But it's Different with Jesus, Right?

But surely the image of Jesus in John 4 is different than earlier images of power imbalances that I began with. Jesus *is actually good*, right? Aren't there many positive stories that have come out of the church's mission in the world? Couldn't this passage be read in a better light? As a church we should not avoid the topic of colonial logic just because we can point to some positive examples of mission. We live with all the consequences of the Christian West's mission to the world that remains entangled in theological and political factors. Within this history, as Mennonites, we have emphasized our hardships but less often do we recall the roles we have played in colonizing land in the Ukraine and Paraguay, as well as here in Canada, and for the benefit of larger powers trying to stabilize their claims. There is no neutral position on these matters. Even if we reject how the church has engaged in mission, we must acknowledge the effects of the past and face the realities of the present.

As I mentioned earlier, Samaritans were considered something like "half-breeds" because they were once the northern tribes of Israel but were invaded and colonized by Assyria. They were no longer pure in the eyes of some of the Jews of Judea. But just as Jesus reopened this once closed story between Jews and Samaritans by walking through Samaria, we also will need to reopen this story found in John 4. We need to consider how this scenario might have played out differently.

A Reopened Ending: Learning the Stories that Bring Life

More important than following the particular "steps" taken by Jesus in this text, we should rather look at the act of reopening closed stories. In the case of the Samaritans, their story was of a people cut off from healing and restoration with their ancestors, the Jews. In this way, John 4 can be read as an account of reopening a story of rejection and condemnation. This reading calls us to be critical of and address how colonial logic can be found in the Bible (even in the Gospels) while still acknowledging the act of reopening closed boundaries based on prejudice and discrimination. From this perspective, it is interesting to place John 4 in the light of other significant biblical and historical events; to see within and beyond the biblical accounts of reopening once closed stories.

- The creation story of Genesis 1 reopened the violent endings of other creation stories in the ancient Near East. As the people struggled with exile in Babylon and were immersed in their creation myth that spoke only of violent competition, the Israelites reopened the story and spoke of the peace that is promised by their God.

- The book of Job reopened the fears people had that disaster meant they angered God. When Job's friends tried to convince him through their orthodox positions of guilt and punishment, Job reopened the conversation, challenging us to call God to account and find how to face God in the midst of our struggles.
- In our generation civil rights leaders and activists reopened the closed story of racism and sexism, demanding that we see how deeply we have cut off certain people and groups.
- Indigenous communities reopened the closed story told to them by Western Christians, a story which too-often declared their bodies and beliefs as inferior to the gospel. Indigenous communities in the West have reopened that story by recovering their traditions and values alongside and outside the church's story.
- The gay community reopened the relationship between faithfulness and love. Being consistently denied a part in the church's story of marriage, this community is forming its own visions of how to love well.

Jesus reopened the closed story between Jews and Samaritans. Where do you find yourself today in relation to the stories of success, health, acceptance, and hope? What are the family and neighborhood stories you bring with you in your journey? What are the stories our church and countries tell? We cannot change all these stories but our mission can be to look for openings; openings to discard and escape the stories that bind life; openings to enter the spaces that bring life. May the God of Spirit and Truth guide us in these ways.

Amen.

The Nothingness of the Church under the Cross:

Mission *without* Colonialism

Ry O. Siggelkow[1]

> *"Indeed, even though there may be so-called gods in heaven or on earth — as in fact there are many gods and many lords — yet for us there is one God, the Father, from whom are all things and for whom we exist, and one Lord, Jesus Christ, through whom are all things and through whom we exist" (1 Cor. 8:5–6).*

The theme of mission is not merely one subset of theology — it is related fundamentally to all aspects of theological inquiry and Christian practice. This is so because to seriously reflect theologically and practically on the theme of mission is to be confronted with the question of the very truth of the gospel itself. On the one hand, this is simply a way of emphasizing what has been the constant refrain of many missiologists over the past half century or so, which may be best summarized in the phrase "mission is the mother of theology."[2] On the other hand, in this article I want to suggest that when one begins to reflect theologically and practically on the theme of mission, one is confronted with questions that run much broader and deeper than what one is perhaps initially prone to see on the surface of things. This is especially true given the current

1 *Ry O. Siggelkow is an adjunct instructor of theology at the University of St. Thomas (St. Paul, MN) and a PhD candidate in theology and ethics at Princeton Theological Seminary (Princeton, NJ). He is a member of Faith Mennonite Church (Minneapolis, MN).*

I am grateful to Christian Andrews, Tyler Davis, Isak de Vries, Kait Dugan, Darrell Guder, and Deanna Womack for their helpful criticisms and comments on earlier drafts of this article.

2 This phrase comes from Martin Kähler. See especially his *Schriften zur Christologie und Mission* (Munich: Chr. Kaiser Verlag, 1971). For a helpful overview of theology of mission in the last century see David J. Bosch, *Transforming Mission: Paradigm Shifts in Theology of Mission* (Maryknoll, NY: Orbis Books, 1991).

"post-Christendom" context of missiological inquiry.[3] To address the theme of mission in a post-Christendom context is not merely a matter of changing missionary "tactics" or "strategies" in the face of a new modern or postmodern situation. Rather, what is especially crucial for theologians and Christian churches to come to terms with today is the way in which the modern history of Christian mission is in many significant respects inextricably linked with the modern history of Western colonialism.[4] This is not a point that can be easily overcome or sidestepped. For what is at stake in this history is the question of the truth of the gospel itself and the extent to which the coincidence of Christian mission and Western colonialism marks nothing less than a denial of the gospel.

It is not enough to merely acknowledge, confess, and repent for the violent colonial history of Christian mission. The pressing task of theology is rather to critically interrogate the theological conditions by which the gospel itself became bound theologically, ideologically, and practically to established powers. Theology is to interrogate how and why the gospel became so bound to established powers to the extent that Christian mission became almost inseparable from the expansion of the Western Christian religiopolitical apparatus which included the colonial propagation of Western sociopolitical, cultural, racial, economic, and ethical norms, practices and institutions. To reflect critically and honestly about this history and the theological conditions that made it possible is central to what it means to think "mission" faithfully today.

All of this is to simply underscore *how much* is at stake theologically and practically when one confronts the question of mission in a post-Christendom context. Never again can theologians, pastors, and missionaries allow the gos-

---

3 See Darrell Guder, *Missional Church: A Vision for the Sending of the Church in North America* (Grand Rapids, MI: Eerdmans, 1998); and Darrell Guder, *The Continuing Conversion of the Church* (Grand Rapids, MI: Eerdmans, 2000).

4 Of course much of twentieth-century missiology has been preoccupied with this very question. For the classic study see Stephen Neill, *Colonialism and Christian Missions* (New York: McGraw-Hill, 1966). See also Lamin Sanneh, *Translating the Message: The Missionary Impact on Culture* (Maryknoll, NY: Orbis Books, 1989). See also the important work of John G. Flett, *The Witness of God: The Trinity, Missio Dei, Karl Barth, and the Nature of Christian Community* (Grand Rapids, MI: Eerdmans, 2010). More recently see the collection edited by Dana L. Robert, *Converting Colonialism: Visions and Realities in Mission History 1706-1914* (Grand Rapids, MI: Eerdmans, 2008). For a helpful discussion of the ongoing significance of the work of Edward Said for contemporary missiology, see Deanna Ferree Womack, "Edward Said and the Orientalised Body: A Call for Missiological Engagement," *Swedish Missiological Themes* 99, no. 4 (2011): 441–61.

pel of Jesus Christ to become captive to the ideology of colonialist and impe-
rialist expansion. In this light, the task of theological reflection thus becomes
a matter of asking after the ways in which the church continues to conceive
of and even carry out "mission" within the framework of these deeply rooted
theological assumptions.

In this article I seek to re-situate the question of mission theologically
within the context of early Christian apocalyptic. This is, in part, a way of taking up and extending David Shank's claim that "the eschatological kingdom
orientation of the Anabaptists remains the essential mainspring of mission
— of Christian messianism."[5] Drawing on the theology of Ernst Käsemann, I
argue that whenever one finds this eschatological kingdom orientation moving
into the background of theology and practice — what Käsemann calls early
Christian apocalyptic — the church as an institution comes to the foreground
as that community which sacramentally mediates and dispenses the gospel and
salvation. What is of particular interest here theologically is the way in which
apocalyptic expectancy and hope for the imminent coming of the Parousia and
the kingdom of God has radically slackened, even vanished, over the course
of Christian history, and the connection this has with the theological shape of
Christian mission in relation to the kingdom of God and the world. The first
contention of this article is that the slackening of apocalyptic expectancy and
hope is, in significant respects, the theological condition for the possibility of
a Christendom model of the church. The second contention is that the history of Christian mission *as* colonialism is bound up with what John Howard
Yoder called "Constantinianism." Indeed, the combination of the slackening
of apocalyptic expectation and the rise of Constantinianism is the condition
of possibility for the equivalence of mission and Western colonialism.[6] Building on Martin Kähler and J. C. Hoekendijk before him, David Bosch rightly
highlighted the ways in which Christian mission within such a framework can
all too easily take the form of *propaganda*. As Bosch defines it, "propaganda is

---

5 David A. Shank, "Anabaptism and Mission," in *Mission from the Margins: Selected
Writings from the Life and Ministry of David A. Shank*, ed. James R. Krabill (Scottdale,
PA: Herald Press, 2010), 293.

6 To be sure, a certain kind of apocalyptic expectation has not been absent from
the history of the Western colonialist imagination. When apocalyptic is divorced from
its christological basis and no longer takes shape as a mode of expectation under the
signum crucis, it runs the risk of becoming supremely ideological. For more on this
point, see Christian T. Collins Winn and Amos Yong, "The Apocalypse of Colonialism: Notes toward a Postcolonial Eschatology," in *Evangelical Postcolonial Conversations:
Global Awakenings in Theology and Praxis*, eds. Kay Higuera Smith, Jayachitra Lalitha,
and L. Daniel Hawk (Downers Grove, IL: InterVarsity Press, 2014), 139–51.

always the spreading of 'Christianity', that means: the gospel plus culture; the gospel plus confessionalism; the gospel plus a set of moral codes; the gospel plus some feeling of ethnical superiority, always resulting in reproducing exact replicas of the sending church."[7] Furthermore, as Hoekendijk claims, the essential characteristic of mission as propaganda is precisely a "lack of expectant hope and an absence of due humility."[8] The constructive section of this article thus seeks to re-situate Christian mission within the framework of apocalyptic expectancy and hope in a way that fundamentally challenges propagandistic and colonialistic theologies of mission.

Despite David Shank's insistence that an eschatological orientation has historically been the "essential mainspring" of Anabaptist theology and practice, there remains a relative dearth of constructive Anabaptist theological engagement with a specifically *apocalyptic* approach to a theology of Christian mission.[9] Thus one of the underlying motivations of this article is to encourage a retrieval of an apocalyptic theological imagination for Anabaptist and Mennonite theology and practice, especially in relation to ongoing theological reflection on the church and its mission. While all the specific theological implications of such a retrieval for Anabaptist and Mennonite theology cannot be wholly determined in advance, in its expectancy for a future that is discontinuous with the present configuration of things, it is my hope that apocalyptic theology will continue the work of problematizing the tendency in Anabaptist and Mennonite theology to stabilize the contours of what constitutes Anabaptist and Mennonite ecclesial identity. Indeed, if Chris Huebner is right to note that Mennonites are in the midst of a "full-blown identity crisis," a retrieval of apocalyptic theology will probably do less to *resolve* this crisis of identity than to call for the validity of its theological permanence.[10] Such a remark is not meant to encourage perpetual ecclesial "navel-gazing" so much as it is a way to emphasize the sense in which the apocalyptic gospel is always *destabilizing*

---

7 David J. Bosch, "Systematic Theology and Mission: The Voice of an Early Pioneer," *Theologia Evangelica* 5, no. 3 (1972), 183.

8 J. C. Hoekendijk, "The Call to Evangelism," in *The Church Inside Out*, trans. Isaac C. Rottenberg (Philadelphia: Westminster Press, 1966), 23.

9 The most important work on the theme of apocalyptic and Christian mission is Nathan R. Kerr, Christ, History and Apocalyptic: The Politics of Christian Mission (Eugene, OR: Cascade, 2008). The Mennonite theologian John Howard Yoder is of pivotal constructive significance in Kerr's genealogy of apocalyptic in modern theology.

10 Despite his critical remarks of a certain tone in contemporary apocalyptic theology, this article resonates deeply with Huebner's insistence that the peace of Christ is "radically unstable and risky precisely because it exists as gift."

of claims to identity, especially attempts to establish the boundaries of *ecclesial* identity. Apocalyptic theology thus serves to challenge the perennial Anabaptist and Mennonite theological temptation to all too readily mark off the visible contours of the faithful ecclesial body vis-à-vis an unbelieving world. The goal of this particular article is to show how apocalyptic theology challenges claims to stable ecclesial identity and in so doing serves to reconfigure and recast Anabaptist and Mennonite theologies of Christian mission.[11]

The Slackening of Apocalyptic and the Rise of the Church as Christendom

Ernst Käsemann famously argued that early Christian eschatology is characterized by the apocalyptic expectation of the imminent coming of God's kingdom, of the Parousia of Jesus Christ, and the dawn of the new creation.[12] For Käsemann this view is especially characteristic of the theology that governs Paul's letters. Yet, within the New Testament itself, Käsemann noted, one can already discern a modification of eschatology, which eventually ends in the "final extinction" of apocalyptic from the dominant forms of Christian theology and practice.[13] With the disappearance of apocalyptic expectation there arises the establishment of the "great Church which understands itself as the *Una Sancta Apostolica*."[14] Käsemann describes this shift polemically in terms of a

---

See Chris K. Huebner, *A Precarious Peace: Yoderian Explorations on Theology, Knowledge, and Identity* (Scottdale, PA: Herald Press, 2006), 36. For his recent criticisms of apocalyptic theology, see Chris K. Huebner, "The Apocalyptic Body of Christ? Reflections on Yoder and Apocalyptic Theology by Way of David Foster Wallace," *Pro Ecclesia* 23, no. 2 (Spring 2014): 125–31.

11 "Apocalyptic" is, of course, a slippery term. While there has recently been a renewed interest in "apocalyptic theology," what constitutes its general emphases and concerns is far from clear. In this article, I seek to extend the tradition of biblical exegesis and theology represented by Ernst Käsemann and the so-called "Union School," which includes such figures as Paul Lehmann, J. Louis Martyn, Christopher Morse, Nancy Duff, Beverly Gaventa, and James F. Kay. More recently, David Congdon, Halden Doerge, Nathan R. Kerr, and Philip G. Ziegler have made notable contributions to this ongoing conversation. For a volume bringing together a diversity of voices on the theme of apocalyptic, see Douglas Harink and Josh Davis, eds., *The Future of Apocalyptic Theology: With and Beyond J. Louis Martyn* (Eugene, OR: Cascade, 2012).

12 While Ernst Käsemann makes this argument most famously in two important essays, "The Beginnings of Christian Theology" and "On the Subject of Primitive Christian Apocalyptic," in *New Testament Questions of Today*, trans. W.J. Montague (London: SCM Press, 1969): 82–107, 108–37.

13 Käsemann, "Paul and Early Catholicism," in *New Testament Questions of Today*, trans. W.J. Montague (London: SCM Press, 1969), 237.

14 Ibid.

transition from apocalyptic to "early Catholicism." And while there is no doubt that Käsemann formulates the issue in terms of a polemical opposition between the "Protestant view" and Roman Catholicism, such clear-cut and confessionally loaded designations cannot be so easily sustained. Rather the issues are deeply internal to Christian theology itself, arising no less in Protestant and even radical Protestant theological traditions than in Roman Catholic circles.[15]

At issue is the way in which the slackening of apocalyptic expectation coincides with the rise of the church as an established institution viewed within a salvation-historical schema, which sacramentally mediates and secures the salvation of its members. While an eschatological framework is not entirely lost from view in this transition, the priority and singularity of Jesus Christ as Lord becomes overshadowed and even submerged into an ecclesiological construct. Consequently, according to Käsemann, the meaning of faith is no longer determined by an apocalyptic expectancy for the Parousia of Jesus Christ but becomes centrally oriented around incorporation into the church community, which is now statically conceived as that state of being in which one becomes an elected member of the Christian religion. Revelation is no longer that action of God which encounters the world as a dynamic event, but is now treated as a "piece of property which is at the community's disposal," which is to be safeguarded and preserved through a traditioned process of handing down orthodox doctrine and practice. Apostolicity is no longer understood in its original missionary sense as the Spirit's sending of messengers of the gospel but is now viewed as the historical source and arbiter of the church's doctrinal tradition. As Käsemann puts it, "The messenger of the Gospel has become the guarantor of the tradition, the witness of the resurrection has become the witness of the *historia sacra*, the bearer of the eschatological action of God has become a pillar of the institution which dispenses salvation, the man who is subject to the eschatological temptation has become the man who brings *securitas*."[16]

In the midst of this eschatological shift, characterized most acutely by the slackening of apocalyptic expectation and the loss of a christological basis

---

15 The point is made not merely out of a concern for good ecumenical manners. The reality is that such a designation simply fails to do justice to the deeply apocalyptic elements of much Roman Catholic theology, perhaps especially highlighted in Roman Catholic liberation theologians of the twentieth century. See especially the contributions of Johan Baptist Metz, Jon Sobrino, Gustavo Gutierrez, Leonardo Boff, and, more recently and forcefully, David Tracy. Moreover, these developments may be judged as legitimate outworkings of the documents of the Second Vatican Council.

16 Ernst Käsemann, "An Apologia for Primitive Christian Eschatology," *Essays on New Testament Themes*, trans. W.J. Montague (London: SCM Press, 1964), 177.

for eschatology, the imminent future now becomes re-situated *within* a salvation-historical process with the established church at the center, becoming the safe-house for the righteous and godly set over against those outside its sacramentally and doctrinally guarded walls.[17]

The priority and singularity of Jesus Christ is submerged into ecclesiology, and discipleship becomes identified with adherence to an objectively given tradition and a "Christian way of life." According to Käsemann, all of this has drastic consequences for Christian mission. The person of Christ is transformed into a mere cipher for an "ideal picture" of human achievement; now the Christian is depicted as "a gladiator in the arena of virtue."[18] The telos of discipleship is to become virtuous, to enter into the glory of God, and to partake in the divine nature by way of deification. The whole of early apocalyptic eschatology is transferred into a Hellenistic dualism which reinterprets the world as split down the middle into the "ungodly" and the "corrupt," on the one side, and the "godly" and the "incorrupt" on the other. The telos of the human in Christ is thus to emigrate from one world to the other by way of the building up of virtue. To have faith now means to be incorporated into the church as an institution, and Christian mission becomes a matter of territorial expansion.

Constantinianism as a Misunderstanding of the Confession "Jesus is Lord"

The slackening of apocalyptic expectation thus coincides with the rise of the established church and an ecclesiology is developed in order to support and preserve the integrity of the church as a community of virtue. This becomes the condition of possibility for a Christendom model of the church, or the settling down of the church with the powers of this world. Such a shift is also closely

---

17 On the issue of salvation history see especially Ernst Käsemann, "Justification and Salvation History in the Epistle to the Romans," in *Perspectives on Paul*, trans. Margaret Kohl (Philadelphia: Fortress Press, 1971), 60-78. Käsemann does not seek to play justification and salvation history against each other but to insist on the "right co-ordination" of the two. Käsemann is concerned to emphasize that salvation history is only properly understood as a matter of God's faithfulness to the ungodly. In other words, salvation history is "paradoxical" because it occurs "under the sign of the World and in the face of Sarah's justifiable laughter" (70). He writes, "Will the crucified Christ which Grünewald painted ever lose its frightfulness? . . . . Christianity has long told a story of salvation which justifies the institution of the church as the community of 'good' people. The muted colors of our church windows transform the story of the Nazarene into a saint's legend in which the cross is merely an episode, being the transition to the ascension — as if we are dealing with a variation of the Hercules myth" (71).

18 Käsemann, "An Apologia," 179.

related to what John Howard Yoder called "Constantinianism." Constantinianism is, for Yoder, not merely a reference to the fourth-century emperor, but a term that refers to a decisive shift in early Christian eschatology.[19] Yoder's description of Constantinianism parallels what Käsemann identifies as the roots of "early Catholicism," or what may better be called a Christendom model of the church. According to Yoder, the earliest Christian confession — "Jesus is Lord" — is an eschatological, even apocalyptic, statement of faith and hope. Such a confession stands in a directly subversive relation to all visible, established powers, whether cultural, economic, or sociopolitical.[20]

But here we must go further still, for the confession "Jesus is Lord" is not *only* a politically subversive confession, it is also an *apocalyptic* confession that is *cosmic* in scope.[21] In other words, for the early Christians to confess "Jesus is Lord" meant not *only* a refusal of the lordship of Caesar, but also a refusal of the lordship of the powers of sin and death — of the rule of Satan.[22] As Käsemann put it, the apocalyptic confession "Jesus is Lord" is an *answer* to the question,

---

19 John Howard Yoder takes up the theme of Constantinianism at a number of different points in his work. It is not uncommon for him to articulate Constantinianism in terms of a historical eschatological shift in the Christian community. See, for example, John Howard Yoder, "Peace without Eschatology?" in *The Royal Priesthood: Essays Ecclesiastical and Ecumenical*, ed. Michael Cartwright (Scottdale, PA: Herald Press, 1998).

20 John Howard Yoder rightly notes that the problem of Constantinianism is not this or that identification of the gospel with this or that established power, but rather the more basic structural error of identifying the gospel with any established power. "Should we not rather," as Yoder helpfully puts it, "question the readiness to establish a symbiotic relationship to every social structure rather than questioning only the tactics of having allied itself with the wrong one?" See John Howard Yoder, "Christ, the Hope of the World in *The Royal Priesthood: Essays Ecclesiastical and Ecumenical*, ed. Michael Cartwright (Scottdale, PA: Herald Press, 1998), 202.

21 Beverly Gaventa argues that what motivates Paul theologically in Galatians is not first of all his interpretation of the gospel's relationship to the law, but the singularity of the gospel of Jesus Christ and the sense in which this gospel marks a sharp antithesis — indeed a crisis — between the new creation and the cosmos enslaved by the anti-God powers of Sin and Death. See Beverly Roberts Gaventa, "The Singularity of the Gospel," in *Our Mother Saint Paul* (Louisville, KY: Westminster John Knox Press, 2007), 103.

22 Of course John Howard Yoder does acknowledge the ways in which the confession "Jesus is Lord" is a crisis to the powers and principalities. At times, however, Yoder is overly concerned to suggest that the confession is reducible to a merely functional significance as that which serves to distinguish the church as an alternative visible political body vis-à-vis an unbelieving world. Further, his appropriation of New Testament eschatology and the powers relies much too heavily on the work of H. Berkhof and O. Cullmann.

"Who owns the earth?" And so, drawing on Käsemann's insights one might push beyond Yoder to say that what is at stake is not merely a recognition of the directly ethical or political import of the early confession, but rather the extent to which such an apocalyptic confession indicated nothing less than the subversion of *the enslaved world*, and so also positions itself polemically against the immanental framework upon which the ethical and the political as such still trade.

To apocalyptically confess "Jesus is Lord" did not amount to the confirmation of established power but rather, we might say, it announced the apocalyptic *crisis* of every established power. Indeed, it was and is the apocalyptic crisis of the world insofar as it is a world enslaved to anti-God powers. What is especially important to grasp here, however, is that this *crisis* was not exactly "visible to all" in any obvious way — indeed, it was visible only under the sign of the crucifixion (*signum crucis*). The confession was a statement of *faith* and of *hope*. While the early Christians believed that the cross and resurrection of Jesus fundamentally and decisively changed reality — importantly, this was based not in the visibility of an objective change in lordship but *in* faith and so was not visible to all. Rome continued to reign, the power of sin continued to hold sway over people's lives and the world generally, and death had pretty clearly not ceased. "Jesus is Lord," then, was an invisible, eschatological reality — it was not any less *true* or decisive for the Christian life, but it was still that for which one stood in hope and in which one believed in faith by the Holy Spirit under sign of the cross. The coming kingdom of God, the new creation, the objectively visible lordship of Jesus Christ was in a very important sense *not yet*, which is why Paul will speak of a creation that still *groans* for the coming new creation (Rom. 8:18–25).

What is perhaps most important to emphasize at this point is the sense in which Constantinianism is a theological misconstrual of this basic Christian confession, and it is a misconstrual that is deeply intertwined with the slackening of apocalyptic expectation, viz., the slackening of faith and hope that the kingdom of God is *at hand* but not *in hand*.[23] Constantinianism is the transposition of the confession "Jesus is Lord" into a process that is now taking

---

While the powers cannot be "restored" to some pristine origin, for the former, they can most certainly be "Christianized" for the common good; for the latter the powers are part of a larger providentially construed salvation-historical dramatic battle. See H. Berkhof, *Christ and the Powers*, trans. John Howard Yoder (Scottdale, PA: Herald Press, 1977), 58–65.

23 See Christopher Morse, *The Difference Heaven Makes* (New York: T&T Clark, 2010).

place visibly, objectively, and publicly in the course of historical events. It is, we might say, a forcible attempt to bring the future into the present — and to identify what is now emerging visibly with the triumphant realization of the kingdom of God in history. But Constantinianism is also marked by a particular way of viewing God's providence in and through the historical process as such — specifically and concretely, it is the belief that the transformation of the Roman Empire into a *Christian* Roman Empire was the action and expression of God's will, the making visible what had only once been believed in faith and in hope (namely, that "Jesus is Lord").

It is precisely at this point, however, that one must critically interrogate the way in which the critique of Constantinianism is too often taken up by Yoder as a way to *prop up* the church itself as a visible political body that is missiologically set over against the world. In Yoder's view, the dire consequence of Constantinianism is that it renders invisible the church–world distinction. For Yoder, this is problematic insofar as it winds up in a fusion of church and world allowing early Christianity to lose sight of the fact that "the meaning of history is in the work of the church."[24] While Yoder is right to characterize "the world" theologically as "structured unbelief," he is wrong to view the church community itself as the bearer of the meaning of history. Such an account radically fails to grapple with the extent to which *structured unbelief* runs through the heart of the church community itself.[25] Indeed, the critical apocalyptic point forcefully made by Käsemann is that Jesus is Lord over both church *and* world, and so "visibility" as a theological category for the church's self-definition is quite wrongly understood if it assumes the place of an unquestioned predicate of the church community itself. Even more problematically, it is precisely this visible church–world distinction, for Yoder, which becomes the theological condition and basis for Christian mission.[26] Within such a framework, mission cannot help become a matter of the socio-political propagation of the church's own visible life, even if that propagation is strictly qualified as a *minority* posi-

---

24 Yoder, "The Otherness of the Church," in *The Royal Priesthood: Essays Ecclesiastical and Ecumenical*, ed. Michael Cartwright (Scottdale, PA: Herald Press, 1998), 61.

25 For more on this, especially on the extremely problematic shape John Howard Yoder's theology has taken in the theology of Stanley Hauerwas, see Ry O. Siggelkow, "Toward an Apocalyptic Peace Church: Christian Pacifism after Hauerwas," *The Conrad Grebel Review* 31, no. 3 (2013): 274–97.

26 See, for example, John Howard Yoder, "Church Types and Mission: A Radical Reformation Perspective," in *Theology of Mission: A Believers Church Perspective*, eds. Gayle Gerber Koontz and Andy Alexis-Baker (Downer's Grove, IL: InterVarsity Press, 2014), 159.

tion within society. Indeed, what is at stake here is the question of a theologically faithful account of the church's visibility vis-à-vis the world.

By way of a critical alternative to Yoder, we might say that the church is visible just to the extent that it witnesses *not* to its own life as the meaning of history, but to the eschatological *life to come* under which both church *and* world stand in permanent, apocalyptic, crisis. The issue is wrongly put when it is posed as a question as to the location of the meaning of history — for the church is not the answer to the question of the *meaning* of history; rather, we might better say that it is the apocalypse of Jesus Christ that is the crisis of meaning in history as such. Thus, we would do well to critically ask after the ways in which there is still yet a latent realized — even *triumphant* — eschatology in Yoder's thought, which plays itself out most problematically in his definition of the church as a sociopolitical body that visibly bears the marks of the life to come and contains within itself the meaning of history.[27]

Mission as Colonialism

The above is, I think, the central logic of Constantinianism and it is this logic which is, in combination with the slackening of apocalyptic expectation and the emergence of a Christendom doctrine of the church, the theological vision that shapes and sustains the modern collusion of Christian mission and Western colonialism. In Constantinian Christendom, and in the theology that undergirds and sustains its vision, the apocalyptic kingdom of God no longer represents a fundamental crisis to established power; far less does the kingdom of God pose any real crisis to the established church. For the kingdom is now triumphantly pulled into the present age, becomes strongly identified with the structures of the institutional church and its tradition as well as the dominant established powers, and Christian mission is transformed into the *churchification* of the world.[28] Such a theological vision of mission is rooted in the theological presumption that the gospel can be neatly aligned with establishment

---

27 John Howard Yoder consistently interprets the doctrine of the invisibility of the church as a way to allow for the possibility of faith outside of visible church boundaries. But this is a very narrow understanding of the doctrine, especially the version developed during the Reformation. For a helpful clarification of this doctrine and its importance, see John Webster, "The Visible Attests the Invisible," in *The Community of the Word: Toward an Evangelical Ecclesiology* (Downers Grove, IL: InterVarsity Press, 2005), 96–113.

28 See Ernst Käsemann, *Jesus Means Freedom* (Philadelphia, PA: Fortress Press, 1972), 99. See also, Hoekendijk, "The Call to Evangelism," 25. "Evangelism and *churchification* are not identical, and very often they are each other's bitterest enemies" (italics original).

political and cultural power without losing its very substance. The historico-political arrangement that we have been calling Christendom grows out of this decisive shift in eschatology, and the slackening of apocalyptic. Consequently, the early Christian apocalyptic hope for the imminent coming of the Parousia of Jesus Christ no longer stands as a "crisis" to every established order; rather it is the church *as* Christendom, identified as a sign and outworking of God's providence in history, which bears within itself the very destiny of the world.

Within this context Christian mission becomes integrally bound up with the continuation, the maintenance, and the colonial *propagation* of a particular sociopolitical, ethical, economic, and cultural order. It is bound up with the maintenance of these orders in a variety of ways: most violently, through "crusades" against that which threatens the integrity of the politicized body of the church, through the excommunication or execution of "heretics," and through the outright annihilation of any and all otherness, anything that would pose a threat to the integrity of Christian cultural and political identity and territory. As Christendom seeks to expand outward into new lands in modern history, there emerges the deadly combination of Christian mission with colonialism, or Christian mission *as* colonialism — once again, the continuation and propagation and also the maintenance of a particular sociopolitical, ethical, economic, and cultural order — what we now call "the West."

Mission *without* Colonialism

As I have stated above, to reflect on mission is to be confronted with the very substance of the gospel itself — part of this confrontation is to honestly view the history of Christendom and the ways in which the logic of Constantinianism has made possible a theological imagination that would carry out crusades and a violent colonial project under the banner of "mission." What is important to realize is that such colonialism is in many ways made possible by deeply rooted theological failures. So, how are we to understand mission in a way that is theologically faithful to the gospel of Jesus Christ? How are we to understand mission in a way that refuses the ideological capture of the gospel by powers that seek to enslave and destroy? In short, what might it mean to rethink Christian mission *without* colonialism?

Because mission is not merely one subset of Christian theology the task is not rightly understood as simply a matter of rethinking mission. Rather the task is to rethink the relationship between kingdom, church, and world in light of a more faithful hearing of the gospel of Jesus Christ.[29] Of course this rethinking does not mean we simply throw out the Christian theological tradition altogether — one must maintain a dialectical relationship to the theological legacy of Christendom.[30] But this does not relieve us at all from the task of rethinking important elements of our theology. In fact, it makes that work much *more* pressing and laborious because it arises out of a deeper and more serious engagement with the Christian theological tradition and the legacy of Christendom. But the reason why we *must* rethink the *whole of it* is precisely because mission is not one subset of theology just as it is not one element of church life. It is a question of rethinking mission apocalyptically as a dynamic *event* which is inseparable from the activity of the sending of the Holy Spirit *in* and *for* the world.

What takes priority in an apocalyptic theology of mission is decidedly *not* the church as an established order that needs to be maintained in order for it to be territorially and politically replicated, propagated, and expanded, but rather the in-breaking activity of God in Jesus Christ in and for the reconciliation and redemption of the *cosmos*. And so it is not so much that the church itself *has* a mission but rather that God is a *missionary* God, a God-in-Action, a God whose face is always turned to the world in grace and judgment — and a God who in the power of the cross and resurrection, calls forth *witnesses*.[31]

To rethink mission in this way is to see the connection between mission and witness as constitutive of *ekklesia* — of church — of the community of those who are called forth to be disciples of the living Lord Jesus Christ and whose lives are precisely as such given over for the sake of a world in bondage to the powers of sin and death.[32] But what does it mean to be so given? What does the church "have" that the world does not have? The answer, it seems to me, is *nothing*. For the church does not possess the gospel! The missionary church that

---

29 For some provisional theses in this direction see Nathan R. Kerr, Ry O. Siggelkow, and Halden Doerge, "Kingdom-World-Church: Some Provisional Theses," from the blog *Inhabitatio Dei*, posted on June 8, 2010, http://www.inhabitatiodei.com/2010/06/08/kingdom-world-church-some-provisional-theses/.

30 I am indebted to Darrell Guder for helping me to better understand this point.

31 As Jürgen Moltmann puts it, "Mission does not come from the church; it is from mission and in the light of mission that the church has to be understood." Jürgen Moltmann, *The Church in the Power of the Spirit: A Contribution to Messianic Ecclesiology*, trans. Margaret Kohl (Minneapolis: Fortress Press, 1993), 10.

32 On sin as a cosmic power see Beverly Roberts Gaventa, "The Cosmic Power of Sin in Paul's Letter to the Romans," in *Our Mother Saint Paul* (Louisville, KY: Westminster John Knox Press, 2007), 125–36.

is faithful to the gospel does not so much give itself to the world — as if the purpose of its mission is to point back to the church's own interior life, as if the church bears within itself something that the world *needs*; rather the missionary church gives itself up *unto* what it is *not* in and of itself, namely the crucified Jesus Christ and the coming kingdom of God. And this is what it means to begin to rethink mission and witness theologically within a post-Christendom context; it is the missionary church that gives itself up unto witness, in an *ek-centric* movement that points away from what the church is in itself by pointing *to* the living Lord Jesus Christ. In other words, the missionary church is that community called forth by God in the power of the Holy Spirit that never loses sight of the fact that its sole purpose and reason for existence is to *witness* to the one who became nothing for the sake of the world, the crucified Jesus Christ, and to say that here, in this mutilated body, is the salvation of the world. "He must increase; I must decrease" (John 3:30).

Mission as Solidarity with the World *under* the Cross

And so, we might say that the church in mission is a church called forth by God in the power of the Holy Spirit to live and to work as witnesses to the good news that, in the cross and resurrection of Jesus, God has reconciled the world to Godself. The church is called forth to witness to the occurrence of this singular, unrepeatable event in history, but the church is not only called forth to witness to this event as something *past*. The church is also called forth to witness to the *promise* of the future coming of God's kingdom.[33] Here, as before, the missionary church is not called to point *back to itself*, nor is it called to point to any established kingdom on earth. It is rather called to point in faith and in hope and in love, in the power of the Holy Spirit, to the future which is imminently and apocalyptically coming. The church thus lives in *expectancy* of the coming of God's kingdom — a kingdom that comes *for the earth*. And the church announces in word and in deed that this future, which is *not yet* here but which is nonetheless promised, marks the final defeat of the powers of sin and death, the passing away of the old world, for it is God's victory over every anti-God power. It is, in short, God's final word of love for the world: the justification of the ungodly and the resurrection of the dead.

Ecclesia Crucis: the Mark of the Missionary Church

Living in the expectancy of this future the missionary church is given to live in

---

33 As Wilbert Shenk puts it, "The promissio of the eschaton is correlated with missio . . . ." Wilbert R. Shenk, *Changing Frontiers of Mission* (Maryknoll, NY: Orbis Books, 1999), 19.

solidarity with this suffering world that God so loves, a world that still *groans* under the weight of the powers of sin and death.[34] By the power of the Holy Spirit the missionary church is thus thrown into the depths of those places *most* marked by the powers of sin and death.[35] And it is for this reason that the missionary church is given to be the church not of the godly, of the pious, of the religious, of the holy, of the saved, but the church of the *ungodly*, of sinners — and so it is to live and to work with and among the damned and wretched of the earth.[36] The church is given to live and to weep among the dying and the dead, the social outcasts, the mentally ill, the prisoners, and especially the crucified peoples of the earth.[37] It is into these spaces of death and nothingness, from these spaces of *hell*, that the missionary church is faithful to its calling to be *conformed* to Christ's own life and death — for his is a life that is always self-emptying and self-expending, a life that transgresses the boundaries of our ecclesiologically constructed notions of "sacred" and "profane."[38] To faithfully witness to this crucified body is to risk the integrity and wholeness of the church vis-à-vis the world; indeed, it is to put at risk the church's perceived "holiness." God moves his witnesses into hell on earth, not heaven, because God loves the whole world *without* exception. And it is precisely here in the midst of hell that the missionary church is given to proclaim that "Jesus is victor!" For there is no hell — whether visible or invisible — that can keep out the

---

34 See Beverly Roberts Gaventa, "The Apocalyptic Community," in *Our Mother Saint Paul* (Louisville, KY: Westminster John Knox Press, 2007), 137–48.

35 For a brilliant description of an ecclesia crucis — a church of Holy Saturday, see Alan Lewis, *Between Cross and Resurrection: A Theology of Holy Saturday* (Grand Rapids, MI: Eerdmans, 2001).

36 "Christians know of the God who will create the new heaven with a new earth, who forever puts down the mighty from their thrones, calls blessed those who labor and are heavy laden, and has become Advocate of all the damned of the earth. If it should be revolutionary to state that the Father of the Crucified is not a God of the possessors and enforcers, for good or ill Christians must take the side of the revolutionaries because they are called to serve humankind and not the partisans of those who cry for order, by which they mean the preservation and continuance of their own power, their traditional prejudices, and their economic, cultural, and political privileges." Käsemann, "The Righteousness of God in Paul," in *On Being a Disciple of the Crucified Nazarene: Unpublished Lectures and Sermons*, trans. Roy A. Harrisville (Grand Rapids, MI: Eerdmans, 2010), 26.

37 See Jon Sobrino, *No Salvation Outside the Poor: Prophetic-Utopian Essays* (Maryknoll, NY: Orbis Books, 2008).

38 See Donald M. MacKinnon, "Kenosis and Establishment," *The Stripping of the Altars* (Bungay, UK: The Chaucer Press, 1969), 13–40.

power of the love of God in Jesus Christ. In the words of Christoph Blumhardt, "God is ready, always ready, to break up any hell."[39]

Mission as Resistance, Service, and Work for Liberation

The missionary church is that community which is called forth by God, the community that lives from Pentecost in the power of Holy Spirit under the cross of Jesus Christ and in expectancy of the promise of the coming of God's kingdom. The Spirit that is poured out at Pentecost is a Spirit *for the earth* — the promised future of God's kingdom is a promise *for all of creation*. And that Spirit and that promise are none other than the gifts of God in Jesus Christ. The Spirit is both a gift and a power that calls forth witnesses — but she is never a possession of the church community or of particular ecclesial offices. The Spirit cannot be packaged or dispensed, nor can she be "handed down" by way of a set of doctrine or traditioned practices — she cannot be ecclesiastically domesticated precisely because God is *free*, and she is free *charismatically*.[40] Yet the Spirit *possesses* us — she lays hold of us individually and corporately — and this occurs as the calling forth of disciples, of witnesses, of those who are brought into the captivity of service, of a new obedience to Jesus Christ. While each one is called by the Spirit to a specific task and vocation, the Spirit is not something that settles down, she cannot be managed or controlled, for she is wildly and creatively *dynamic* and always moves with great power as she quickens and announces her presence by calling forth obedience, by calling forth disciples. Because the Spirit is not a predicate of the church community, and because the Spirit is inseparable from the nothingness of the crucified Jesus Christ, one might also say that, theologically speaking, the missionary church is that community which holds nothing in common.[41] It is also to say that the work of the Spirit is the dispossession of the church community of any and all

---

39 Christoph Blumhardt, *The Gospel of God's Reign: Living for the Kingdom of God*, trans., Peter Rutherford, et al.; eds. Christian T. Collins Winn and Charles E. Moore (Eugene, OR: Cascade, 2014), 13.

40 "Evangelical freedom cannot be bureaucratized." In Käsemann, "Beginning of the Gospel: The Message of the Kingdom of God," in *On Being a Disciple of the Crucified Nazarene: Unpublished Lectures and Sermons*, trans. Roy A. Harrisville (Grand Rapids, MI: Eerdmans, 2010), 13.

41 Cf. Alphonso Lingis, *The Community of Those Who Have Nothing in Common* (Bloomington, IN: Indiana University Press, 1994). "The community that produces something in common, that establishes truth and that now establishes a technological universe of simulacra, excludes the savages, the mystics, the psychotics — excludes their utterances and their bodies. It excludes them in its own space: tortures" (13). (*continued*)

claims to private property.[42]

The charismatic action of the Spirit is not that which takes us out of the world to stand over against the world as the established triumphant church — she is not that which consecrates certain times, places, or offices as "holy" and "sacred" — she is rather that power which moves us into the service of Jesus Christ for the world, seeing the world anew in light of God's action in Jesus Christ, again and again, as if for the first time. Such charismatic action occurs as a work of service for the world. But this work of service is neither accommodation nor the confirmation of the world as it is in itself; rather, charismatic action is a work of judgment, a matter of "discerning the spirits," and so also a work of resistance against anti-God powers.[43] As we see in the gospel accounts with Jesus and his disciples, it is a work that involves casting out demons in the power of the Holy Spirit and entering into a spiritual and bodily struggle against every anti-God power, as one is given to announce in word and deed the gospel news that even now as the community in service to the world awaits the future of God's kingdom, God is apocalyptically at work to bring forth life from the dead. Thus charismatic action is marked by the work of service and resistance — a work of struggle especially with and among and alongside those who are continually struck down but nonetheless continue to resist the anti-God powers that enslave the world. It occurs wherever and whenever demons are cast out, wherever and whenever the sick are healed and the blind see, it occurs wherever and whenever prisoners are set free and the oppressed are liberated. Such action, such work, is the sign of the coming of God's kingdom — the passing away of the old world — it is what Paul calls charismata, and it is inseparable from God's dynamic mission in and for the world to make all things new. The missionary church is faithful to God's mission only and insofar as it points exclusively to the one crucified on Golgotha, who was made nothing for the sake of the earth, and to the coming of God's kingdom which comes in power, apocalyptically, to make all things new.

(continued) See also the helpful philosophical reflections on the "no-thing" that constitutes community in Roberto Esposito, "Appendix: Community and Nihilism," *Communitas: The Origin and Destiny of Community*, trans. Timothy Campbell (Stanford, CA: Stanford University Press, 2010), 135–49.

42 Cf. Dietrich Bonhoeffer, *Letters and Papers from Prison, Dietrich Bonhoeffer Works English* (Fortress Press, 2011). "The church is church only when it is there for others. As a first step it must give away all its property to those in need" (503).

43 "Resistance is the reverse side of faith. Those who believe live unavoidably in strife with the powers ruling this earth." Käsemann, "The Righteousness of God in Paul," 23.

Mennonites and Theological Education among Indigenous Churches in Ecuador:

A Perspective from the Last Two Decades

CÉSAR MOYA[1]

Introduction

One of the ministries supported by the Mennonite Partnership for Ecuador — which includes Mennonite Mission Network (MMN), Iglesia Menonita de Colombia, and Central Plains Mennonite Conference — involves supporting theological education among indigenous evangelical churches. This article presents a historical sketch of theological education supported by Mennonites among indigenous evangelicals in Ecuador from 1991 to 2010.

In this article I will describe how paradigm changes were carried out, moving from an evangelical approach imposed from the outside, to one more informed by indigenous ways of thinking and acting, shaped also by the challenges of liberation theology. Coincidentally, these paradigm changes took place when Anabaptist theological perspectives were taught through several courses and workshops, in alliances between Mennonites and other institutions that share a common goal of supporting theological training for evangelical indigenous churches.

I present here more personal reflections of what I noticed through my experiences in theological education with my wife, Patricia, as well as my thoughts upon reading a few written sources. My reflections are pulled from courses and conversations with pastors, leaders, students, teachers, and indigenous communities from 1995 to 2010. I will begin with a few antecedents, and then will

---

1 *César Moya currently teaches at Mennonite Biblical Seminary in Colombia, and is also a PhD candidate at the Vrije Universiteit Ámsterdam. Moya served in Ecuador with Mennonite Mission Network and in partnership with Colombia Mennonite Church and Central Plains Mennonite Conference over the past fourteen years. He and his wife, Patricia, served as academic resources in several institutions while in Ecuador, including the theological training program of Ecuadorian Federation of Indigenous Evangelicals (FEINE) and Indigenous Center of Theological Studies (CIET).*

briefly present the methodology, dimensions, characteristics, and the results of theological education among indigenous groups, concluding with some of the challenges before us. I recognize every aspect of this article deserves further development in future work.

I hope this article generates a profitable dialogue between Mennonites and indigenous people about the *Missio Dei* (the mission of God), especially among those who serve in the field of theological education.

Antecedents

The arrival of evangelical missions

The establishment of formal theological education in Ecuador coincides with the arrival of evangelical and Protestant mission initiative towards the end of the 19th century. Once mission groups settled themselves and had followers, they began to create biblical institutes in order to train the first local pastors and church leaders. It was not until the the middle of the 20th century that a more organized and systematized method of theological education emerged.

The majority of indigenous evangelical churches were established by the Gospel Missionary Union with the support of other mission agencies such as HCJB ("The Voice of the Andes," a Christian missionary radio station in Ecuador) and the Summer Institute of Linguistics. These established churches — the majority of them evangelical but not belonging legally or administratively to any missionary organization — influenced indigenous communities in their lifestyle habits, particularly in the lives of the men. So, abstinence from alcohol and tobacco, for example, improved the quality of family life. Indigenous communities also, however, assimilated Fundamentalist Christianity that was brought by North American missionaries of different denominational backgrounds, resulting in isolation from political life.[2]

---

2 Fundamentalism is a complex phenomenon that merits further explanation. For the sake of this article, I refer only to the movement that originated inside North American Protestantism, and existed in evangelical settings in the 20th and 21st centuries. Its name is derived from five "fundamental" assessments that its founders promulgated in a meeting in Niágara in 1895: 1) the inerrancy of the Bible; 2) the virgin birth of Jesus Christ; 3) the doctrine of substitutionary atonement; 4) the bodily resurrection of Jesus; and 5) the imminent personal return of Jesus Christ. See Justo González, *Diccionario Manual Teológico* (Barcelona: CLIE, 2010), 129–30. Fundamentalism is part of evangelical Protestantism that influenced Latin American churches, resulting in divisions both in the traditional churches and the Pentecostal churches, as well as starting new conferences. See José Míguez Bonino, *Rostros del Protestantismo Latino-americano* (Buenos Aires: Nueva Creación, 1995), 35–56.

Doctrinal instruction and its diffusion

Evangelical faith spread through biblical institutes, initiated in 1953 with the objectives of reproducing dogmas and doctrines in the mission churches, as well as teaching church administration. Presently, the institutes are in Quichua hands, but under the mentoring of North American missionaries.

In the 1970s, stories and teaching material on the life of Jesus, evangelical hymns, Bible course modules by extension, and materials on evangelical doctrine were published in indigenous languages. Music institutes were also created to teach people how to play instruments, sing, and compose hymns. In 1985 an institute was opened to train religious teachers in the transmission of evangelical doctrine to children in congregations.

Until the end of the 1980s, the content of doctrinal instruction generally included:

- Bible studies with emphasis on memorization and literal interpretation;
- Dogmatic emphases with eschatological and messianic content;
- Moralistic evangelical ethics;
- Procedures for liturgical celebrations;
- Program divisions according to gender — some for men and the others for women;
- Affirmation and defense of pastoral ministry exclusively for men — a teaching sustained in an androcentric and patriarchal interpretation of the Bible; and
- No academic requirements to enter the programs — just a calling from God.

Despite these perspectives, many indigenous evangelicals were instructed and became pastors with strong Christian commitments.

Yet how was it possible to reproduce such doctrinal instruction in a region characterized by high mountains, cold weather, and lack of good roads, as was the case of the Chimborazo province? Few things would have been possible without the Colta Radio Station, created in 1931, and the Voice of the AIIECH (Association of Evangelical Indigenous Churches of Chimborazo), whose wavelengths were transmitted to evangelical indigenous communities within its reach.

The Journey towards Change

We have seen how the theological education among indigenous churches followed models that reproduced dogmas and doctrines, some of them influenced by fundamentalist movements. But, beginning the 1990s, other paradigms appeared in theological education through two institutions: the Ecuadorian Federation of Indigenous Evangelicals (FEINE), with its headquarters in Quito, and the Indigenous Foundation for Development (FUIDE), with its headquarters in Riobamba. These organizations, both in relationships with Mennonite agencies, initiated a gradual breakdown of the traditional theological paradigms, which had prioritized doctrine over life and dogmatism over the community hermeneutic.

FEINE arose in the early 1980s with indigenous evangelical church associations from different regions of the country, with social as well as religious purposes, and in a time of fervour for agrarian reforms. Many of these associations were headed by Monsignor Leonidas Proaño, the principal promoter at the time of liberation theology among the indigenous communities of Chimborazo.

In the early 1990s, more than half of the 2,800 indigenous churches in the country did not have either trained pastors or church leaders. During this time, FEINE entered the national political scene and invited Mennonite Board of Missions (MBM, the predecessor agency of MMN) to support them in biblical and theological training. Over the last fifty years, Mennonites had successfully supported the development of unique theological training methodologies in indigenous churches in both Ivory Coast and Argentine Chaco.[3]

A result of this invitation was the establishment of an agreement in 1993 between AIIECH with the MBM and the Latin American Biblical Seminary (which today is the Latin American Biblical University, or UBL) in Costa Rica. This partnership resulted in the birth of the Indigenous Center of Theological Studies, with headquarters in Riobamba. This center was charged with developing programs of theology and ministry, and inspired by liberation theology. In the first year it enrolled nearly two hundred students. Particularly from 1993 to 1997, and afterwards, various indigenous evangelicals in Chimborazo were able to advance in their theological training in Ecuador, while others went to Costa Rica with a scholarship.

As a result of this theological training, some students created various programs with FUIDE: one for theological training (which became a satellite

---

3 The experience in the Chaco in Argentina is told by Willis Horst, Ute Mueller-Eckhardt, and Frank Paul in *Misión sin conquista: Acompañamiento de comunidades indígenas autóctonas como práctica misionera alternativa* (Buenos Aires: KAYROS, 2009). Several reflections about the experiences in Ivory Cost are told by James R. Krabill in *Is it Insensitive to Share your Faith? Hard Questions about Christian Mission in a Plural World* (Intercourse, PA: Good, 2005).

of the Latin American Biblical University), a scholarship program, and later, a project assessment program. Indigenous evangelicals who graduated from the UBL immediately became resources for teaching in the university-level theological education program.[4] However, in 1997 the new board of AIIECH stopped calling for the academic formation of religious leaders and the development of an indigenous theology, labelling the contents of courses as liberation theology. In spite of everything, UBL and MMN maintained their support of Indigenous Center of Theological Studies (CIET).

Later, theological education continued through the Pastors' Council of FEINE, which, along with FUIDE, received the support of the Latin American Council of Churches (CLAI), MMN, and the UBL, in order to train in a direct way at an intermediate level more than one hundred pastors and leaders, both men and women. Sixty graduated from 2001 to 2005. At the same time, a new university-level extension of the UBL in Quito was opened. It was based in the Methodist Church and had twenty students from different denominations,[5] including five indigenous students,[6] one of whom finished her bachelor's degree in theology in Costa Rica.[7] This effort generated confidence among these institutions that signed an agreement in order to support more than 140 pastors and indigenous leaders during the period 2007 to 2009. Most of them graduated from the intermediate and beginner levels in November 2009.

As we can see, paradigm changes in theological education were carried out through the efforts of several entities — some of whose perspectives were liberal, and others liberationist, and along with FEINE and FUIDE — whose leaders had the openness to change their theological perspective.

Developed methodology

During the last two decades, indigenous theological education developed methodologies through trial and error. There has not been one single pedagogical method, rather, methods have evolved and adapted to changing situations. While the implementation of theological education awakened great interest in the university program in the early 1990s, indigenous students were not at high enough education level to make use of formal theological education. Because

---

4 These were Julián Guamán, Gerónimo Yantalema, and Margarita de la Torre.

5 The students belonged to the Lutheran, Baptist, Mennonite, and Methodist Churches, the Salvation Army, and various indigenous churches.

6 Two of which are leaders in FEINE — Willian and Rafael Chela.

7 This student was Blanca Viracocha, a youth leader with the Methodist Church in the Pastocalle Township, in Cotopaxi province, and who belonged to the Romerillos community.

of this greater attention has been given to beginner and intermediate levels.

The intermediate level has followed the 24 modules of CEPA (the Pastoral Education Course) of the UBL, whose methodology follows the "see, judge, act" method.[8] In spite of the practicality of these modules, after several years of use it was recognized among the same indigenous peoples that this was not the most appropriate method for them, given their levels of education and how they processed concepts. In spite of that, intermediate-level teachers continue to use the modules as a guide, making adaptations in their classes to help facilitate interactive learning.

Given that indigenous recognized the modules of CEPA had a higher academic level for them, in 2007 the Pastors' Council of FEINE found it necessary to begin developing a biblical, theological, and pastoral training program at the beginner level, making use of a methodology and content that call for indigenous evangelical peoples to move from being *objects of* to *subjects engaged in* theology. The program consists of twelve courses, made up of four workshops per year, with three courses per workshop. This curriculum was developed over the course of six events and from a Latin American theological perspective.

In the first event a series of workshops was held with twenty pastors and leaders who had completed FEINE's program in previous years. These workshops touched on the Ecuadorian context, transforming education, indigenous worldviews, and the creation of popular-level contextual curricula. In the second event, a set of criteria was developed to determine topics for the curriculum, define its content, and define recurring themes, among them nonviolence, justice, gender equity, ecology, and ethnic diversity. At the third event, appropriate content and pedagogical methods were defined for each topic. In the fourth, biblical, theological, and pastoral starting points were proposed. During the fifth event, booklets were created for each one of the twelve topics chosen as urgent and necessary. And the final event was the evaluation after the first year, which produced feedback in some of the content and applied methodologies.

The twelve booklets that were created were on the following topics:

1. Conflict resolution from a biblical perspective;
2. Church administration for the 21st century;

---

8 This method was initiated by the Second Vatican Council and has been used by the Base Ecclesial Communities. It means: starting from the historical reality of our world (see), illuminate this reality with God's word (judge) in order to begin a new practice (act). See Victor Codina, *¿Qué es la Teología de la Liberación?* (Bogotá: CINEP, 1988), 15–20.

3. Financial administration in the church;
4. Community pastoral accompaniment;
5. Celebrate a service to the God of Life;
6. Communication of the word of God in the community;
7. Announcing the kingdom of God;
8. Contextualized Christian education;
9. The reasons for our faith;
10. Reading the Bible with different eyes;
11. Jesus as the model for leadership; and
12. The church and social development.[9]

There are other booklets currently being created on topics suggested by the same churches and communities, including for example church and polity, church and state, gender equality, the Ecuadorian context, and indigenous worldviews.

During the creation of these booklets and the implementation of the program, indigenous pastors and leaders from different provinces on the national level have played an active and decisive role in each stage. They have developed criteria taking into account the needs of the churches and communities; they have chosen the most urgent and necessary topics, identified learning techniques from their own culture, chosen pertinent biblical texts to illuminate particular situations from their reality, shared their own experiences from their rural and/or urban contexts, identified an appropriate learning process for the students in each one of the topics, and they have been facilitators in the majority of the courses. My role in the process consisted of assessing pedagogy and theology.

The workshop participants have expressed their appreciation for how the program has helped them read the Bible with different eyes, challenging them to think about how to engage in pastoral ministry that addresses contexts of poverty, exclusion, and marginalization. The program has encouraged them to be instruments of transformation and liberation in their situations of oppression.

Dimensions of Indigenous Theological Education

When I refer to 'dimensions', I mean the relational areas of the human being in which an indigenous theological education aims to work. Thus, when reviewing the last two decades of theological education among indigenous evangelicals in

9 See FEINE, CLAI, MMN, *Programa Pastoral Indígena: Cartillas de formación bíblica, teológica y pastoral* (Quito: CLAI, 2010).

Ecuador, which has operated with non-traditional paradigms, one can identify the dimensions illustrated in Figure 1.[10]

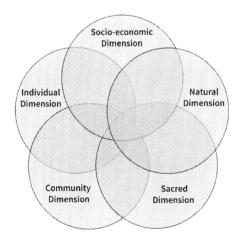

Figure 1. *Dimensions of Indigenous Theological Education*

The sacred dimension

The sacred dimension is the area of theological education that is articulated in relationship with the Creator. It is evidenced in the conception of God, the Creator, as revealed through the Bible, human beings, Christ, the church, nature, and the events of everyday life. Indigenous communities are profoundly religious, and this aspect circulates in all areas of life, from the individual to the social-political, the present and the future, life here and that which is beyond. All that happens around them is explained with reference to the supernatural. However, even though everything is integrated in the spiritual, a separation between the sacred and the profane is observed.

The social-political dimension

The social-political dimension is the relational area where indigenous communities intersect with the social and political transformation of the nation, region, or community where they live. They understand political life to be tightly related to all of life, and it is seen as the will and revelation of God for history.

---

10 This proposal is inspired by the correlation method of Paul Tillich in *Systematic Theology*. I, II, III (New York and Evanston: University of Chicago and Harper & Row, 1967).

The natural dimension

The natural dimension is reflected in two principal ways. First, native peoples have profound respect and care for creation, reflected in their methods of cultivation and their affectionate treatment of animals. This dimension conceives of Earth as Mother, as *Pachamama*, "because she is who gives live, food, drink, and clothes. She is part of my life, and my life is part of her. There is a link; from her we came, we are part of her, and to her we will return, as it says Gen. 3:19."[11] And second, the natural dimension is evidenced in the human relationship with the rest of the environment, including water (which is like *Pachamama*'s blood), vegetation, mountains, sun, moon, and stars — all are part of the cycle of each human being.

The individual dimension

The individual dimension pertains to practices (both moral and ethical) that help determine an appropriate lifestyle. Here enters the triple prohibition: *Ama shua* (do not steal), *Ama quilla* (do not be lazy), and *Ama llulla* (do not lie). When an individual must be admonished, it means the community has failed. However, this individual dimension also demonstrates how well the individual communicates with nature and with God, and how he or she understands the message forwarded by them. This dimension shows the relationship of each individual with their Creator. Because of this *shamanes* or *yachais* (wise men and women) are recognized in the community as people with special qualities of relating deeply with God and spiritual forces.

The community dimension

The community dimension is evidenced in each person's generosity and concern for neighbor, companion, sibling, and friend. This includes the community of faith as well as the community or town of origin. The community is the extension of the family. Mother earth exists in the functioning of the community, and the community is fulfilled in relation to the earth. On behalf of the earth, *mingas* — community work days — are organized around planting and harvest. Additionally, a worldview of reciprocity exists that is connected to the future, more than to the present, a person, or a specific community, and is characterized by giving from what one has with joy, and not from what is leftover.

The dimensions listed above are integral to indigenous worldviews and spiritualties. As noted, the individual is tightly interrelated with the sacred, social-political, nature, and the community (ecclesial or otherwise) to which he or she belongs. As such, theological education should be carried out recog-

---

11 This is the interpretation of Willian Chela.

nizing this interrelatedness. In other words, theological education must be a holistic process. The teacher or facilitator thus becomes very important, because they must live out all the previous dimensions in order not just to be accepted by the students or communities, but also to be models worthy of imitation. The teacher should not just have academic knowledge, but should actually integrate the five dimensions in their life. Because of this, it is difficult for Westerners to serve as the best people for this process. It is better for teachers from the same indigenous groups to serve in their communities, as they will operate from similar worldviews.

Characteristics of Theological Education in Ecuador

The new paradigms of theological education that were implemented in Ecuador during the 1990s and the first decade of the 21st century (a period of Mennonite involvement) have specific characteristics, as outlined below.

Strategic alliances

Theological education has been developed with new paradigms thanks to strategic alliances between indigenous evangelical associations, biblical and theological educational institutions (such as the UBL), and ecclesial institutions such as CLAI and MMN. In these alliances a *minga* — community work group — of students, teaching resources, economic resources, administrative resources, and academic resources has been created. Indigenous ways of working are respected in these alliances, considering indigenous peoples as subjects rather than objects.

Priority of Scripture in doctrine

An indigenous friend once said, "If through the Bible slavery and fundamentalism entered into our communities, it is with the same Bible that we will achieve liberation."[12] Many good indigenous customs were abandoned because of prohibitions taught to them, and due to misinterpretations of Scripture. For example, some communities were prohibited from playing indigenous instruments. Another harmful teaching was that indigenous peoples were taught to be silent, even when experiencing grave injustices, like when their women were abused by the landowners. Some instances of Scripture being misinterpreted came about, in part, because of the biblical translations being used. Despite having Bible translations in different local languages, such as Tsáchila, Quichua, Shuar, and Cofán, among others, the Bible that is most used is the

---

12 Quoted from Gerónimo Yantalema in a meeting in what was previously known as Indigenous Center of Theological Studies.

Spanish Version Reina-Valera, with the *Nueva Versión Internacional* being second. These translations are often preferred, if only because Spanish is the most common shared language, even though, with some exceptions, principally in the Amazon, interpreters with at least three languages are required.

Oral methods

The best teaching methods, in spite of the different didactic techniques learned in various courses, continue to be oral. Facilitators can spend hours speaking without losing the attention of their audience. This methodology should be filled with anecdotes and life stories for illustration.

Recurring topics

Theological education has tried to recover appreciation for indigenous worldviews, and, given cultural patriarchy, it has been important to insert topics of gender equality, nonviolence, and ethnicity.

New paradigms

The rupture of traditional paradigms has occurred. The former evangelical paradigm is being replaced by ecumenical and interreligious paradigms, deliverance from spirits by holistic liberation, exclusivity by inclusivity, inequality by equality, anthropocentrism by ecological care, and that of androcentrism by gender equality. These new paradigms were inspired in Latin American theologies and other liberal theologies.

Latin American facilitators

In contrast to the other programs of theological education, the new theological training programs have been facilitated by Latin American personnel, the majority of them indigenous, especially at the beginner and intermediate levels.[13] This has helped indigenous peoples have their theology grow out of their contexts.

Intergenerational

Theological education is for people of all ages and generations. There are youth, young adults, and older adults all in the same class. There is no age limit to participate in courses provided. This creates trust and dialogue between the present and the past. This differs from the Western conception where there are

---

13 The teaching personnel supported initially by MBM and later by MMN have been Latin American, with formation and appreciation for Anabaptist and Latin American theology. The first were Mauricio Chenlo and Sara Padilla between 1992 and 1995, followed by César Moya and Patricia Urueña from 2000 to the present.

requirements linked, many of them, to age.

Intercultural

These programs of theological education have included persons of different Ecuadorian cultures, such as Quichuas, Otavalos, Shuars, Ashuars, Salasacas, Cañaris, and Saraguros, among others. This diversity is enriched with the participation of *mestizos* — people of mixed ancestry.

Inclusive

In addition to the various cultures, the educational process has included individuals with certain physical challenges such as blindness, speech impediments, and physical problems. This provides different perspectives in the classroom, and challenges the creativity of the instructors.

Minimal logistical structure

This educational process has used the resources which are available in each community where the courses and workshops are held. Fields, a potato crop, or the shade of a tree provide settings for instruction.

Results

Some results of this theological education developed among indigenous evangelicals in the last two decades are apparent and include:

- The promotion and raising up of social and educational projects, which are presumed to be part of the mission of the church.[14] Examples include FUIDE, in Riobamba, and *Ñuchanchic Yachai* ("our wisdom") school, in Cebadas.
- The raising up of leaders with political and administrative capabilities. We emphasize the presence of several former students in decisive political posts, as well as those serving as leaders of institutions who encouraged the process of theological education.[15]

---

14 We want to emphasize the creation of FUIDE as well as the bilingual intercultural school "Yucanchic Yachai" in the Cebadas Township, Guamote County, province of Chimborazo.

15 It is important to mention Julián Guamán, who won the Citizens' Participation Commission's contest, a regular representative of the State, having presided during an assigned time, as well as Marco Murillo, President of FEINE, and Gerónimo Yantalema, ex-director of FUIDE, members of the National Assembly elected by popular vote in the elections of 2010. It is equally worth emphasizing the nomination, among other councilors, of Humberto Toapanta, youth leader of the indigenous church in Saquisilí, province of Cotopaxi.

- Capability of dialogue at a national level. It is worth highlighting the recognition of FEINE as a political interlocutor through different governments.
- The participation of women in theological education, in the same programs as men, and the openness of some churches to accepting women in pastoral ministry.[16]
- The bi-vocationalism of certain leaders, in which the study of theology encouraged them to thoughtfully engage in other professions.
- Social and political activism of indigenous evangelicals, who were once considered in other social sectors and political movements as illiterate and ignorant.
- Openness to ecumenical dialogue due to the participation of indigenous Baptist, Lutheran, and independent churches, as well as teachers from mainline Protestant churches.
- Involvement in political movements, where the people have been able to offer the voice of their communities. Theological training offered tools to indigenous evangelicals to become involved in the struggles for recognition and the promotion of the rights of their peoples.
- Social mobility as an expression of being attentive to what is happening in Ecuador. This has become a priority reflected in worship services and evangelistic activities.

Conclusions and Challenges

Theological education among indigenous evangelicals in Ecuador in the past two decades (supported by Mennonites, among others), broke the traditional paradigms which prioritized doctrine over life and dogmatism over the community hermeneutic. This effort began with the participation of people linked to associations of indigenous evangelicals from certain regions, especially in Chimborazo, with the participation of FUIDE and FEINE. These efforts have been accompanied by the UBL, MMN, and, in the last six years, CLAI, having left certain significant results for the indigenous evangelicals. Even though there are still several traditional Bible institutes, most of them are convinced by this theological education perspective since they were under FEINE's struc-

---

16 Manuela Gualán, in Chimborazo, and María Otavalo, in Imbabura, were recognized as pastors less than a year ago, according to information obtained by Pastor Pedro Sisa, interim president of FEINE and president of the National Council of Pastors, as well as Willian Chela, youth coordinator of FEINE.

ture.

Even though the development of indigenous theological education has taken nearly twenty years, it still needs to mature. Persistence and indigenous evangelical leadership convinced of the value of these efforts for their communities, churches, and the country are required. The formation of indigenous theologians who from their own contextual experience and worldview are able to make biblical rereadings appropriate to their situation must be encouraged. Additionally, persistence and patience are needed in those who accompany these educational processes through the ups and downs that occur along the way, in financial as well as organizational issues.

Even though many indigenous evangelicals have been changed by this new Latin American theological perspective, those who aim for management positions in the organizations are those who have been most resistant to a Latin American perspective. This creates uncertainty concerning the continuity of the program.

The tension that exists between the need for leadership training and autonomy of the indigenous ecclesial communities constitutes a challenge for educational processes. Even though these partnering institutions wish to respect indigenous ways of thinking, there exists an outside influence, whether in methods or content. Because of this, accompaniment should be carried out with careful judgment and sensitivity so that the errors of the past are not repeated.

Additionally, there is need for the recovery of indigenous ancestral values and traditions which have been and are being lost from generation to generation, primarily due to urban migration.

The tension that exists between educating theologically with methods and contents which do, and those which do not, exist in their culture should be recognized. The latter are conducive to a loss of rootedness and the longing for more training, as well as the desire to live like mestizos. This tension increases alongside the technological globalization that has arrived even in the most hidden corners of indigenous communities.

Belong, Believe, Behave:

Reflections on Church Planting in Germany

SHARON BRUGGER NORTON[1]

Reflecting on fourteen years of experience planting Mennonite churches in Germany, the influence of Paul Hiebert's centered-set approach cannot be understated. This reflection will focus on how this approach shaped our church planting team's strategy and practices. Additionally, the concept of "belong, believe, behave" and its effect on our relationships will be explored, including both advantages and challenges encountered. Most of this reflection will center on the church plant in Halle, Germany, which we named "Soli Deo" (from the Latin phrase soli Deo gloria, or to God alone be the glory, based on our belief that if a church is indeed planted, God alone gets the glory).

"German Mennonites don't plant churches," I heard from time to time during my tenure as a church planter in Germany from 1994 to 2008. Thanks to the vision and determination of German pastors like Herbert Hege, some German Mennonites, however, did plant churches, and invited young adults from the United States to join them. Hege contacted Eastern Mennonite Missions (EMM) to ask if a YES team[2] could come to southern Germany to help plant a Mennonite church, and my husband Steve and I were the leaders of that first team in 1994.

Soon after arriving and getting to know Hege, his wife, and their eight children, along with other church members, Steve and I were invited to return as missionaries to focus on planting a church in Pfullendorf, a small village of about twelve thousand that was predominantly Catholic, with varied levels of commitment and involvement in the life of the church. In the summer of 1995, we attended EMM's summer training event called World Missions Institute in Philadelphia, as well as a program called "School of Witness," a three-month summer program of EMM's Discipleship Ministries department. It was that

---

1 *Sharon Brugger Norton served in Germany with her husband and three children from 1994 to 2008, appointed by Eastern Mennonite Missions and later jointly appointed with Mennonite Mission Network. She now is employed by Mennonite Mission Network as Radical Journey Director and as Personnel Counselor for International Ministries.*

2 YES stood for Youth Evangelism Service but now is no longer referred to as an acronym.

summer when we first were introduced to cultural anthropologist Paul Hiebert's description of ecclesial structures by EMM's administrator/missiologist, David Shenk. He explained the terms bounded-set, centered-set and fuzzy-set to us as ways to think about what a church focuses on in its structure.[3] This theory was a major factor shaping our identity as Anabaptist church planters in a post-Christian and postmodern secular society, first in the southwest corner of Germany and later in the eastern part of Germany.

Briefly, the bounded-set focuses on the boundaries, on defining who is in and who is out, and what people must exhibit in their behavior and beliefs in order to belong to any given group. Typically there is an emphasis on holiness and purity. The centered-set defines a few characteristics that are central, and does not focus on the boundaries. People can be any distance from the center and still belong to centered-set group, as long as they are facing the center. We were taught that the center is Jesus and that there are multitudes of ways to experience Jesus, while growing in faith that may look very different, depending on a whole variety of factors, such as upbringing, the surrounding culture and sub-cultures or the religious background of a person. Instead of defining the boundaries, the centered-set focuses on Jesus as the center of our faith and our relationship with him. The fuzzy-set is basically more about belonging to a group without clear definition of boundaries or a clear central focus.

After spending nearly four years in southwest Germany with the church plant there, Steve and I were asked to journey to Halle, an industrial city of about two hundred thirty thousand in the heart of former socialist East Germany, and restart a church plant there. For a variety of reasons, the original church planters had left and it was determined by the German Mennonite Mission Committee and EMM that a second team would go and would be free to use a different strategy than the former team. Again, we attended World Mission Institute in Philadelphia with our new team made up of Jimm and Kaylene Derksen, with their three-year-old daughter, Helena, and Jochen Riehm, a young German man who had found the Mennonites through peace work in Bosnia. Other Americans and Germans joined the team in the following years. Our team was taught the principles of Hiebert's work on bounded-set/centered-set/fuzzy-set and we were encouraged to embrace the centered-set, with Jesus as the center, as we went about planting an Anabaptist church.

Upon arriving in Halle, our team quickly determined that the legacy of a formerly socialist country is quite different than a capitalistic society. Going

---

3 Paul Hiebert, *Anthropological Reflections on Missiological Issues* (Grand Rapids, MI: Baker, 1994), 107–136.

back all the way to the Enlightenment's dismissal of religion as superstition, and the desire for scientific explanations of reality, many people were ready for socialism and were truly heartbroken when the German Democratic Republic (GDR) was dismantled in 1990, and was reunified with former West Germany. Some of the legacy of socialism was atheism and a complete disdain of religion. Churches were turned into museums, concert halls, and, in some places, into forgotten storage buildings for the city. In some more rural areas, genuine Christian faith did indeed continue to exist, but in many of the larger cities, like Halle, only a small minority of the public claimed any Christian religious identity. In fact, in Halle, the registered Christians of all creeds were a little less than 7 percent. We met many people who personally knew of no practicing Christians, or who remembered the odd Christian student who was made fun of in class for their faith. Perhaps there was a distant elderly relative who attended church services and was more or less humored by the family.

Based on these observations, the team decided that we needed to find concrete ways to practice the centered-set structure. But how? We already knew that people generally had no interest in joining a church, or even setting foot inside a church building, so there was no point in starting typical Sunday worship services inside a building with which people had no connection. Doing the slow work of establishing relationships and authentic friendships seemed like the best way to make a start. Members of our team practiced hospitality in our homes, went to the park with our children, joined a book club, taught English, and had many barbeques in our backyard with neighbors and new friends. Eventually, as we practiced sharing our lives, including how our relationship with Jesus affected everything from major life decisions to parenting and finances, some people became curious and wanted to know more. Some people were clearly not interested. Since we were not concerned primarily with how close or far from the center (Jesus) people were, we chose to walk with anyone who showed signs of turning toward Jesus, which took much time and intentionality.

As people grew in their commitment to walking with Jesus, we encouraged them to deepen their commitment to the community of faith as well, to serve with their gifts and invite others to join them on the journey. We began introducing our new friends to each other and at different times were able to organize groups that focused on certain topics or life-stages, many of which took place in people's homes. At some point there were enough people that it seemed like a weekly gathering for corporate worship, teaching, and fellowship would be beneficial. Again, our focus was not on defining who was allowed to come to this gathering, but on making sure everyone felt welcomed, no matter how far or close to the center they were, or even if they were facing toward or away from Jesus. We chose a format that affirmed a German cultural form of hospitality, Kaffee und Kuchen (coffee and cake) on Sunday afternoons. It felt a lot less intimidating to people to be invited to coffee and cake than to be invited to church.

One person who joined us on the journey with Jesus was Anett. She described her childhood as one of neglect and had been turned out at age sixteen to fend for herself, only given the most rudimentary set of household supplies mandated by the government for parents to supply when "emancipating" their sixteen-year-old children. She married young and had a daughter while living in an abusive marriage relationship. After surviving a knife attack by her husband, she left him and raised her daughter on her own. She was unemployed for many years and her daughter was a teenager when we came to know them through her daughter's friends. Anett had a hard shell and was very skeptical of anything to do with God and religion. Over time, however, she started showing up for cake and coffee more often and got to know this strange mix of people who laughed, sang, prayed, and ate a lot of good food. As she shared her life story with us piece by piece, she was able to see how God was in her life even when she did not know it was God. She learned to pray and to forgive, and that hard shell was penetrated by the love of God and God's people. She remains a loyal and faithful member of the church to this day.

The space we met in also was important. As a way of demonstrating Christian community and relationships, the team began living in an abandoned business building along a busy road not far from the city center. There were several apartments and rooms for a meeting place, a kitchen, and a children's room. As a bonus, there was a courtyard large enough for our barbeques to continue! We did not want the space to look "churchy" because of the negative view of churches and church buildings, so it was helpful to be able to focus on Jesus and relationships and not have to overcome the unnecessary burden of having a building that reminded people of their negative perceptions.

One year at our annual EMM Europe retreat, a missionary couple from the Netherlands shared a concept they had heard about: "belong, believe, behave." This paradigm, first coined in writing by Mennonite missiologist and church historian, Alan Kreider, was another way of thinking about the process of conversion and inclusion in the body of Christ. It fit well with the concept of the centered-set, where the primary focus at the beginning is on creating a space for belonging.[4] Genuine relationships must be established and new people must know they are valued and cared for, as they are, with all of their issues, bad habits and messy lives; then one can expect that in this context of love and acceptance, they will be more open to responding to the love of Jesus and will begin to believe. Over time as they grow in faith and relationship with Jesus and other Jesus-followers, some of those bad habits will be transformed. Areas of sin and temptation will be overcome as they see other people overcoming the same. Eventually their behavior will look more like an imitation of Christ. Again, the focus was not on defining clear boundaries concerning belief and behavior, but on the journey of conversion.

As an Anabaptist, embracing the centered-set and "belong, believe, behave" paradigms felt very natural, in large part because of the emphasis Anabaptists put on the centrality of Jesus. How simplifying it was to focus on the Gospel stories of Jesus and introduce this Jesus to people who had never heard, which refreshed long-standing Christians' connection with Jesus as well. How freeing to stop judging people and doing boundary maintenance, and instead letting the Holy Spirit be the one to convict people of their sins! But it was not without challenges.

It was messy to live with the outworkings that a centered-set approach brings. Sometimes it is comforting or appears easier to have a group identity based on people behaving properly as a group. Clear definitions of what is right and wrong also can be comforting to some people. Letting go of religious forms and traditions that could not be directly related to the person and ministry of Jesus was at times a struggle. Some people who had been Christians for years felt like we were far too loose in our theology and allowed far too much bad behavior in our church. It took determination not to revert back to a bounded-set approach and to offer repeated explanations to people who did not understand.

It was not uncommon for couples in Halle to be unwed, but cohabitate and have children together. We were faced with a dilemma of couples in this situation who were becoming interested in following Jesus and yet had many negative stereotypes of marriage. As church leaders, we struggled knowing when to ask these couples to get married. Should we tell them to get separate apartments or to sleep separately if they were not ready to get married? How much pressure should we put on them to marry, and what consequences would we set if they chose not to marry? Instead of focusing on setting policies or thinking up consequences, we kept loving them and talking with them about

---

4 Alan Kreider, *The Origins of Christendom in the West* (Edinburgh: T&T Clark, 2001).

God's intentions for marriage. Eventually they came to realize that it was a next step in their faith journey to marry and those weddings were always a highlight in the life of the church. But in the meantime, it was messy explaining to other Christians that we had unmarried couples living together in our church for significant lengths of time.

While we rejoiced with Anett and learned to love and worship with unwed couples, we learned that people who had been Christians for many years as adults had the most problems with the messiness of our church since that is not what they were used to. The people most happy with our approach were those who had no church background and were positively surprised by "church" not looking like the negative propaganda they had been exposed to in the days of the GDR.

In a setting where the vast majority of the population had little to no experience with churches or Christians, the centered-set approach and the "belong, believe, behave" paradigm worked very well. They facilitated a focus on relationships over rules. They gave room for the gospel to be contextualized in that setting. They were conducive to an environment of curiosity and learning and for conversion to be about a journey over time with people and a God who loves you.

Taking the Longer View

Jeanne Zimmerly Jantzi[1]

Often, Mennonite Central Committee (MCC) measures the end results of its work at the end of three-year project cycles. Only the impact of MCC's specific involvement is measured. As people who've been working with MCC in Indonesia for quite a long time, my husband, Dan, and I are coming to realize that we have a rather unique vantage point in which to appreciate the longer view, or to see the way that God has been working his purpose out over time and through multiple interactions in a particular place.

In late 2012, after twelve years, we handed over our former role in Indonesia to new MCC representatives and moved on to a new role. As our successors work with new projects in Indonesia, we have the opportunity to tell the background stories for these new initiatives. We find these stories to be a fascinating web of interesting connections. It's not just any one seed that was planted, but a result of multiple interactions and acts of God over the years.

In April 2013, MCC partnered with the Javanese Mennonite Churches in responding to seasonal flooding in Central Java, Indonesia. The flooding only affected eight villages, so the disaster hardly registered in national Indonesian news let alone in international news. In the village of Njleper, the community and local church began responding immediately using their own resources, but the needs soon became beyond their ability to cope. In this village of sixty-five families, all of the homes, places of worship and schools were flooded under two meters of water. The newly harvested rice crop was sodden and began to rot. The fish farming ponds overflowed their banks and lost all their fish. The houses, mostly made of wood and bamboo, were severely damaged. After they set up a tent camp, a second flood came, causing the people to need to flee a second time to higher ground.

This type of disaster is often overlooked by the government and by local and international humanitarian organizations. It's too small for them to bother with. And yet this type of disaster is a major crisis for the people who live there and who are most affected. These small responses are where MCC is best able

---

1 *Jeanne Zimmerly Jantzi, and her husband, Daniel Jantzi, currently serve as Mennonite Central Committee Area Directors for Southeast Asia, which includes Laos, Cambodia, Vietnam, Indonesia, Myanmar (Burma), and Philippines. She recently completed twelve years as Mennonite Central Committee's Representative to Indonesia.*

to work alongside the church to fill a niche that no one else is filling.

The Javanese Mennonite Synod planned an initial one-week-long emergency response. Within that time frame, thirty-five families received a packet of emergency supplemental food items sufficient for a one-week period. They didn't need full nutrition rations because people from neighboring villages that had not flooded were bringing vegetables and other food items to share with the flood-impacted families. Twelve of the most vulnerable families with small children or elderly members received mattresses. Sixty-five flood-affected homes were cleaned, along with two public buildings and five places of worship. Those were the outputs or results. But those results don't tell nearly the whole story of God at work in that response in the community of Njleper.

In the longer view, this particular disaster response by the Javanese Mennonite Church was quite significant. In Central Java, many Christians live carefully as a minority among the Muslim majority. While one of the other three Anabaptists denominations (the Muria Mennonite Synod) has led the way in their approach to interfaith issues, the Javanese Mennonite Church has taken a more insular stance, with a history of laying low in order to survive and concerning themselves with caring for their own members.

The disaster response was planned together with the whole Njleper community — both Muslims and Christians. The planning was coordinated by Yunarso Rosadono (Dono for short), a young Javanese Mennonite church leader and kindergarten teacher who was a participant in the YAMEN program in 2007–2008. YAMEN is the Young Anabaptist Mennonite Exchange Network of Mennonite World Conference and MCC. Dono first served in Egypt, and then, in 2008, Dono returned to the Javanese Mennonite Church, which had overcome great challenges over the past thirty years. The church struggled through twenty years of conflict among church leaders causing a split in the large denomination of over 43,000 members. In 2001, the opposing parties reached a reconciliation agreement, with the help of mediation provided by MCC. From 2001 through 2012, the church synod board continued to struggle with legal issues and trust issues that were left as a legacy from the years of conflict. It was difficult for church leaders to think creatively and proactively as they struggled simply to survive as a church.

When Dono returned to Indonesia in 2008, seven years after the official reconciliation, his church synod leaders were reluctant to give him any responsibilities. He was young, he wasn't an ordained pastor, and his ideas seemed too new and different. In addition, the church leaders were spending most of their time in court over disputes about church property from the time of the conflict. Not giving up, Dono sought out opportunities to lead and serve within his local congregation.

Three and a half years later, in 2012, MCC hosted an Asian Anabaptist Diakonia gathering in Indonesia. The Javanese Mennonite Church appointed Dono to attend as one of their two delegates. The other delegate, Hermintono, had been an MCC Indonesia staff person in the 1990s before leaving to become a Javanese Mennonite church pastor.

The Diakonia gathering was an important initiative. In the past, Anabaptist churches in Asia have primarily defined "diakonia" as caring for the widows and orphans within their congregations. The goal of the gathering was to strengthen an Anabaptist theology of diakonia that would result in inclusive, effective service and disaster response actions that would include peacebuilding goals.

The gathering included participants from Indonesia, Vietnam, Japan, Philippines, India, Nepal, China, and South Korea. Three of the speakers — Paulus Sugeng Widjaja, Daniel Listijabudi, and Paulus Hartono — were from the Muria Mennonite Synod in Indonesia. These leaders have frequently interacted with the global church over the years. At this gathering, I took special notes of what these Anabaptist leaders had to say to other Asian Anabaptists.

In speaking of the shared Asian contexts of multiple religions, poverty, and frequent natural disasters, Paulus Sugeng Widjaja said, "Brothers and Sisters, we should not give the privilege of that 'calling-to-respond' to only Western people."

Daniel Listijabudi said: "Diakonia is the struggle to enlarge the circle of neighborliness . . . . It is through service that we respond to the story of what God has done for us."

Paulus Hartono, another Mennonite World Conference and community leader from Indonesia, said, "We live among 100 million Muslims. They won't read the gospel. We must be the gospel in our lives so they can read the gospel in our lives . . . . Transformative diakonia is about relationships. If we have good relationships, where we can talk with each other, then it reduces the risk of violence. We can use words, not violence."

In the Asia Anabaptist Diakonia Conference, Dono and the other delegate from the Javanese Mennonite Synod were encouraged by the opportunity to network with other Anabaptists from around Asia. They were poised to act. However, Dono and others with the vision to "enlarge the circle of neighborliness" still had no official permission from the leaders in the church to begin responding to disasters as a mission of the church.

Then, one more change happened that laid the groundwork to make the disaster response in Njleper possible. The Javanese Mennonite Synod elected a new board in the summer of 2012. This is the first new church board since 2001 that has no members who were involved on either side of the past church conflict. The new General Secretary of the Javanese Mennonite Church, Pak Slamat, is completing his Masters in Peace Studies at Duta Wacana Christian University. The Masters in Peace Studies program developed through the influences of Indonesian Anabaptist academics such as Aristarchus Sukarto and Paulus Sugeng Widjaja, who, in turn, have participated in an international Anabaptist cross-fertilization of ideas. From 2006 to 2008, MCC partnered with this Christian university in providing the funding to launch the Masters in Peace Studies program, the first of its kind in Indonesia. The Peace Studies courses also draw on the experiences of MCC partner organizations by inviting active peace workers to speak to classes as guest lecturers.

The Masters in Peace Studies program provided an opportunity for critical thinking and theological reflection for Pak Slamat. Today, in the large 170-year-old Javanese Mennonite Church, which usually kept a low profile as a survival strategy, leaders like Pak Slamat are talking about the "prophetic voice of the church" and the potential for "transformative diakonia" — the idea that service takes us beyond differences and can be a powerful force in God's kingdom.

This new church board finally gave the go-ahead for Dono and Hermintono to form a church department specifically for Diakonia to the broader community — to Muslims as well as to Christians. So in April, when the flooding happened in Njleper, the church responded with accompaniment from MCC. In the short term, sixty-five households received food support or assistance with clean-up for their homes. That number included fifty-nine Muslim families and six Mennonite families. The minority followers of Christ reached out to expand the circle of neighborliness to include their Muslim neighbors.

In years past, when we or earlier MCC workers carefully planned with partners for the Global Family program, the International Volunteer Exchange Program (IVEP), YAMEN, or Serving and Learning Together (SALT) exchange programs or the scholarships for church leadership development or for the Asia Anabaptist Diakonia Conference or for the launching of the Peace Studies program, no one could have predicted the exact long-term results. As Jesus said in the parable of the sower in Matthew 4: "the seed would sprout and grow, the sower does not know how." The kingdom of God is full of mystery and we, as MCC workers participate in that mystery.

These are not outcomes that have been logically framed or carefully orchestrated to bring change in a predictable way. These are the unforeseen fruits pointing to God's work through the church and through MCC. The unfolding of God's story is amazing to watch because it is bigger than the sum of the short-term results.

On the Way to Living Globally

WALTER SAWATSKY[1]

The following personal reflections, presented in November 2013 at an Anabaptist Mennonite Biblical Seminary (AMBS) mission and peace colloquium hosted by Ted Koontz, were part of a series he and I had sponsored in recent years, by inviting senior persons to reflect on how they had been changed in thinking and living. I of course said yes to Ted's request, but that did not mean I was ready for reflection, or had gained sufficient distance from the experience. The fact of my official retirement in 2012 is still too fresh, and my 'to do' list still too long, for me to offer broad reflections on my life and ministry in peace and mission matters.

In the last issue of *Mission Focus: Annual Review* (2012) that I edited, I included a paper I presented to the 2011 Council of International Ministries (CIM) consultation on ministry in Eurasia entitled "Serious Mission Partners in Eastern Europe: Reflections on 20 Years of Post-Communism." That paper actually addressed general missiology issues for the same time period, so I have avoided repeating myself in what follows. It may be a better clue to why Anabaptist vision, post-Christendom, anti-Constantinianism, or a peace theology applied only through the church barely surface here — those frames of reference were never central to the Mennonite legacy I am speaking from.[2]

At the presentation I introduced several display items to stimulate imaginations, starting with a Russian wooden doll popular in 1988, which showed then USSR President Mikhail Gorbachev, inside whom was Leonid Brezhnev, inside whom was Nikita Khrushchev, inside whom was Josef Stalin, inside whom was Vladimir Lenin, and at the heart of it all was Karl Marx — a vi-

---

1 *Walter Sawatsky is Professor Emeritus of History and Mission at Anabaptist Mennonite Biblical Seminary, where he directed the Mission Studies Center and edited* Mission Focus: Annual Review *and* Religion in Eastern Europe. *Sawatsky served as East-West Consultant for Mennonite Central Committee from 1985-2010.*

2 The north European Anabaptist movement I am referring to here, most specifically its Russian Mennonite expressions (1789–1989), I described elsewhere as one of the many faces of Anabaptism in mission. In a chapter of Andrew Klager's forthcoming *Historical Seeds of Mennonite International Peacebuilding* (Wipf & Stock), my focus is on that tradition's peace legacy. See also my "Menn. Mission und Missionstheologie", in the revised "Mission," Band 2 (http://www.mennlex.de/doku.php?id=top:mission&s[]=missionstheologie, 2013).

sualized legacy then being set to one side, but still a legacy with a continuing impact. Andrei Rublev's famous icon of the Trinity often served me as presence in class to help us think of the relationality of God Father, God Son, and God Holy Spirit, and for a free church audience such as a Mennonite one, to make us more aware of our over focus on Christology — often I asked when last someone had concluded a prayer with the formula "in the name of the Father, Son, and Holy Spirit, Amen" — virtually always used by Orthodox, Catholics, and Protestants alike in the Slavic world.

Indeed, at the time of the celebration of the millennium of Christianity in Slavic lands, widely circulated copies of Ilya Glazunov's 100 Centuries painting served to tell the story. Reading that painting became a lesson in modern ways of seeing/reading an icon. Glazunov's first version of 1988 conveyed a persistent pacifist theme, centered on the innocent Tsarevich and a devuchka (young girl), and even Leo Tolstoy stood at the culminating end of a long row of political cultural leaders, Tolstoy wearing a placard spelling out "nonresistance" to make the point (Image 1) . But only five years later, in a chastened version about the dramatic transformations, the eye was drawn to the young man, now holding a gun, and the innocent girl now his admiring supporter, while our eyes noticed the virtually naked woman dancer, plus shady politicians and business types dealmaking, while in a little bubble Glazunov's self-portrait appeared as the innocent wondering what went so badly wrong (Image 2) . What follows relies on scholarship which set me thinking, but those visual images serve as imagination triggers to remember that lived realities in constant change are the legacy we convey in spite of ourselves.

The Osmosis of Childhood

My mind was often changed on the way to learning to live globally. A few "aha" moments may be of interest to Mennonite readers. I am also trying not to repeat remarks from several other more ceremonial events at the time of my retirement in 2012.[3]

First I must begin with a deep sense of thankfulness for my immediate family. Already on my way to Goshen College in 1965, I knew that I would buy an engagement ring in order to propose to Margaret at Christmas time back in Winnipeg. We were married in the summer of 1966 just before returning for my final year at Goshen for a degree in history. It was the first of three rounds

---

3 More detail to make sense of briefer remarks here come through in chapters by John A. Lapp and N. Gerald Shenk about my career, as published in Mary Raber and Peter F. Penner, eds., *History and Mission in Europe: Continuing the Conversation* (Schwarzenfeld: Neufeld Verlag, 2011).

of obtaining an American visa, the first the easiest, even though Margaret had to work for cash as cleaning staff at the college, while also taking some courses. The next time around was in 1985 when we obtained visas for Margaret and me, not for our daughter Natasha who had been born in Minneapolis during grad school days, but for our son Alex who had been born in London, England. The three of us repeated that waiting game in 1990. Thankfully there was an immigration amnesty so by 1991 we had started part two of my ministry life as seminary professor and East–West consultant for MCC.[4] Thereafter both children married, both having graduated from Goshen College, then received advanced degrees, and now there are five grandchildren, a boy and girl for Alex and his wife Wendi, a boy, a girl, and a baby for Natasha and her husband Aaron Kingsley. Along the way both children also spent time in other countries as we had imagined our own overseas experience had preprogrammed them, but now are settled in Goshen and Winnipeg — two crucial shaping locations for our lives.

I always knew myself as born into a peoplehood, part of the Russian Mennonites who had immigrated to Canada and USA two generations before me, and as part of smaller Mennonite denominations who had split over the pace of spiritual renewal (as they understood it) or the pace of cultural adaptation that I became more aware of as a historian with a social theory minor. My maternal grandfather, Wilhelm H. Falk, was already elected a minister in the Sommerfelder Mennonite community, before he began listening to Mennonite Brethren and General Conference revival preachers, and someone from the Salvation Army. So he experienced a personal conversion, or at least a renewal of an owned piety that transformed his preaching and his desire for a more missionally oriented church. Things came to a head in 1937 when the Sommerfelder leaders rejected him and three other like-minded preachers, so at a subsequent gathering in the village of Rudnerweide they organized the Rudnerweider Mennonite Church, with Falk as the bishop. My father's conversion from the Sommerfelder, where his father had been a respected chorister, had resulted in his baptism by the bishop of the Bergthaler Mennonites, who had separated from the Sommerfelder in an earlier renewal about fifty years earlier. But he fell in love with Bishop Falk's daughter, transferred his membership upon marriage, and within a year was elected minister. It turned out that my father was among the first ministers to move to the city of Winnipeg, where he organized a congregation for other young families leaving the farm for wage earning in

---

4 From January 1990 to August 1991 I commuted between Elkhart and Winnipeg, since the seminary suddenly needed my classes, and the family stayed in Winnipeg until normal immigration was possible.

Image 1. Ilya Glazunov. **Eternal Russia**, *1988. Canvas, oil. 3 x 6 meters. Photograph provided by the author.*

Image 2. Ilya Glazunov. **Russia, Awaken!**, *1994.*
Canvas, oil. 4 x 2.5 meters. Photograph provided by the author.

the city. A dozen years later, having fostered the formation of a conference structure with program boards, etc. my father decided to leave Winnipeg, in order to finish a BA (in history it turned out, with John A. Lapp the primary teacher) at EMU in 1970, when I was already in grad school doing European and Russian history. When he returned to Winnipeg, even though he had been widely respected and loved as pastor and conference president, that conference did not offer him a position, worried how education might have changed him. Several years later, after he had survived running a hardware store and taught at Steinbach Bible College, he became the first conference minister for that same Evangelical Mennonite Mission Conference (EMMC) — another innovation.

That may be more background data than necessary, but it is my way of saying how much I was shaped by osmosis. I never learned to think of ministers and bishops as different from farmers and workers in work clothes, and the many visitors to our house brought their worlds to our table. At our house we talked church, we talked church renewal, we talked mission vision and peacemaking. When my father returned from a trip to the West Indies, the most important line I remembered was his discovery that missionaries were people too, who engaged in petty conflicts and needed outside counsel. I also got the message to study as long as I could — my grandfather's interest in the world, my father's curiosity in new things became a legacy for me. It was surely many years later as scholar and teacher where I more self-consciously rated a capacity for curiosity as essential for ministry, a mindset that expects change and tries to make sense of it.

Changed by Continuous Rethinking of Theology and History

In hindsight I also remember the fear, particularly of being changed fundamentally by more schooling. That first Christmas break from Goshen College in 1965, I attended a meeting of the EMMC Christian Education Commission, where a high-school teacher, with whom I had often shared such meetings earlier, asked whether I was the same Walter, or had college changed me. "It is the same Walter," I said, not only lying but also wondering how he as educator could frame his question that way. That year I had indeed taken a course in sociology of religion that had been transformative.[5] Ever since I have followed the progressions of Peter Berger's thinking about faith, having wrestled deeply with his Invitation to Sociology book, and its section on role theory. I have

---

5 The course, taught by J. Richard Burkholder, his first time I discovered later, plus another the next year by new professor Theron Schlabach provided the blessing of their new thinking (and watching their later development as friend and colleague) to set me on a path of regular rethinking.

watched other students get caught up in the Enlightenment enthusiasm, like philosophes of the 1700s, only two or more centuries too late, and then not getting past that enthusiasm for the rational. My getting to a nevertheless of faith, after wrestling with relativity theory, and the scholastic hubris of thinking one can understand religion and faith phenomenologically, helped me to pursue my curiosities about Marxism — the early theory, its role in Russian intellectual history, and its degeneration when it became official bureaucratic socialism — then to agonize with a brilliant philosopher in the Institute of American Studies (Moscow) who was active in peace matters. He could no longer respect his daughter who had become a conformist official Marxist to get ahead with her career, and instead he envied his son, who had encountered Orthodoxy through priests like Fr. Alexander Men — a man of deep, simple faith, but widely read intellectually — and was now risking his career by coming out as Christian. Yet in spite of his goodwill, and the experience of his youth as exchange student through Brethren Christian Service, he still felt unable personally to make the leap of faith existentially. Within six months of that conversation, he died of a sudden heart attack. My college time leap of faith experience at the same time allowed me, without a sense of inauthentic posing, to enter fully into the fervent faith of the Russian Evangelicals — the old Babushki who blessed every youth showing up for worship — and to discover very savvy urbanites and intellectuals in that same church, who were wishing for opportunities to talk over their faith issues, including how to respond to Orthodox seekers from the intelligentsia.[6]

The primary peoplehood shaping for me was to learn the Mennonite story. It was the story of a pilgrim people, who had been forced to move for conscience' sake. Among vague early memories are hearing C. F. Klassen and his brother-in-law Peter J. Dyck report on the postwar refugees. Whether to immigrate or to stay was always part of the conversation, because some had been rescued from the Communist threat, and others were living or losing their faith under persecution pressures. I also learned the story of the Mennonites from books, first in German, then I recall reading and discussing G. H. Williams' Radical Reformation tome with my father. Throughout, what began to disturb me more deeply was the way the Russian Mennonite story, indeed the

---

6 Two decades later I discovered that a number of those young Evangelicals had experimented with becoming Orthodox (Fr. Men's group and the seminary in Zagorsk), then returning to the Baptist Union after discovering Orthodoxy's shadow sides, but retaining friendships and common reformist commitments. One Mennonite, Vasili Fast, stayed Orthodox and became a priest and theology teacher, while his brother emerged as a key leader of Mennonite Brethren in Kazakhstan.

Anabaptist–Mennonite story, was told from an insider perspective, and was far too idealized compared to what I knew about those people. So when I settled for historical studies, my initial intention was to find the sources for a fuller Mennonite story, to grasp its light and shadow sides.

Among the serendipities of my time in graduate school was the fact that a fellow Canadian Mennonite, Lawrence Klippenstein, chose to focus on Mennonite pacifism in Russia, and that my doctoral adviser, Dr. Theofanis Stavrou, caused my Christian history understandings to expand to new terrain. He liked to describe himself as one born and raised in Cyprus, who did not become an Orthodox priest as expected, but through the Presbyterian missionaries came to USA, where he married an evangelical Presbyterian and began to learn Protestant ways, and to teach us with religious sensitivity. For a time there were ten doctoral students, all working on dissertations connected in some way to the Orthodox East — a very rare religious studies focus in Russian studies at the time.[7] Throughout my life, not only have I retained close fellowship as historian and as Christian with Theofanis Stavrou, but also with many of those doctoral students, and with a few others from other universities, who have been my colleagues in nineteenth- and twentieth-century religious studies ever since. They included Baltic and Swedish Lutherans, Ruthenian Uniates, Greek Orthodox, Roman Catholics, Methodists and Baptists — all comparing those traditions within the Russian Orthodox milieu of what has long been a multi-confessional empire.

I soon realized that focusing on Mennonite history for a dissertation would not adequately unlock the keys to the impact of the Russian setting. It was formative not only because it allowed a fleshing out of early Dutch Anabaptist ideals, but also the Orthodox ethos, the type of state formation within which the Russian Mennonites were essentially the first to develop a spectrum of institutions for ministry and mission, and the surrounding sectarian world influenced them. So I began reading about the sectarian traditions, a research area only recently getting serious attention. But in order to understand the state officials, and their operative theologies, it was obviously necessary to study the history of Russian Orthodoxy. That too was, and largely still remains, an inadequately researched subject. That is truly sad for the West, as well as for the Russians themselves, because it involves a story of centuries of suffering under Muslim dominance, then enlightened despots' aping of the West through subordination

---

7 My dissertation, titled "Prince Alexander N. Golitsyn (1773–1844): Tsarist Minister of Piety," unpublished (University of Minnesota, 1976), was essentially focused on the impact of the eighteenth- and nineteenth-century Pietist movement on Orthodox, Catholic, and Protestant traditions, on Tsarist administrative and educational history.

of Orthodox structures to the modernizing state, and most recently the Soviet experiment that resulted in millions of martyrdoms. If there had ever been any sense of the Mennonites having suffered more than others for their faith, a notion I still encounter rather often, those exposures to a bigger world and its longer story forced me to differentiate more carefully.

Immersed in a Bipolar World

In the early 1970s, North American Christians, including Mennonites, were in tension over whether to support the underground church in the USSR, or the official church. Peter Dyck, then MCC Europe director, learned of a new Centre for the Study of Religion under Communism, based in south London, and visited it. He liked the fact that they were trying to collect data on the whole spectrum of religious life, and were avoiding partisanship even though the director, Michael Bourdeaux, had published books on the dissident Baptists and their leader, Georgy Vins. Soon after Peter Dyck came to visit us in Minneapolis, having learned from his brother, C. J. Dyck, then on the MCC board, that I was finishing a degree in Russian history. So on behalf of MCC he invited us to go to London, England, as an MCC-sponsored research scholar. We intended to serve for three years, which stretched to twelve, nine of them in Germany, from where it was easier to do oral history interviews with recent immigrants and to travel to Eastern Europe and the USSR. As that evolved, we became convinced of the necessity to cross the East–West barrier for the sake of peace, to design programs that placed students in East European settings. So crossing the East–West border for the sake of encouraging persons bearing Christian witness in settings of societal and state hostility to Christians and to other religions turned out to be a long-term ministry, and a long-term learning experience. Much of this we were able to do openly, but without publicity, with the negative result that the supporting constituency was less stimulated to walk with us.[8]

My appointment, and several events soon after, caused me to realize the extent of the culture war Mennonites were caught up in. I was soon treated as a fellow leader to help us navigate the tricky terrain. If my work involved drawing attention to violations of religious rights, tracking the persons imprisoned for reasons of Christian conscience, and making this public, then part of

---

8 That is the central critique in Mark Jantzen, "Tenuous Bridges over the Iron Curtain: Mennonite Central Committee Work in Eastern Europe from 1966 to 1991," *Mission Focus: Annual Review* 18 (2010): 70–90. The article describes many varieties of bridging experience, but did not address the longer story with reference to the USSR, which is probably a central red line in the MCC story till about 2000.

my church community treated me as right wing anti-Communist; when my work involved researching and writing about the officially tolerated Christians, Orthodox included, or to participate in religious and secular peace congresses, then another part of my church community treated me as a socialist liberal. Since this partisanship was also something I encountered among church leaders and educated scholars, I became much more sensitized to how much societal prejudices shape our churchly thinking.

Throughout my time as primarily MCC scholar and administrator, there was always some form of accountability group with whom I met. During virtually every trip to North America, a roomful of Mennonite leaders would meet with me in Winnipeg, Canada, or in Akron, PA, or in Chicago at Council of International Ministries meetings, or on special speaking trips to California and the Canadian west. Always, one group would be anxious not to cause trouble to relatives still in the USSR, warning us not to be too gullible about East European peace overtures, whereas another group pushed for more human and religious rights advocacy, and more testing of ways to have a ministry of presence in Eastern Europe.

As my role evolved into a more explicit church ambassador role, I spent much more time with European Mennonite leaders seeking ways for shared initiatives. After a decade I began to sense that I was noticing their ways of thinking better, coming to know and appreciate the deep differences that were the fruit of national reshaping as French, Swiss, German, and Dutch Mennonites. My language facility had improved too — I was catching more of the nuances, the body language even. The deepest gradual reshaping of my thinking was to realize how often I now asked myself why these Mennonites, or the Protestants, Catholics, and Orthodox with whom I was involved in peace initiatives, were still Christian. All cultural and societal trends seemed to be contrary to Christianity, and the Germans in particular had developed a profound sense of betrayal by the state church institutions which had submitted to the pagan idolatry of National Socialism. To be Christian there was a deliberate choice.

I began noticing and reading more about the reemergence of a people's church from below, the type of people who then showed up in the thousands (and still do so) in annual church days (*Kirchentag*) during Pentecost weekend. Sitting on simple cardboard boxes, hunched together in small groups over morning Bible study, listening to theological sermons where the issues of the day were addressed prophetically, and talking through the many service opportunities offered to them in a market of opportunities, or taking in some seminar, plus evening mass meetings with major speeches, were also for Margaret and me a spiritual refreshing. Today Catholics and Protestants take turns organizing and hosting what is now an ecumenical church weekend. That also caused me to see the much larger real living church than our rhetoric here in America about a secularized Europe allows for, since that usually serves to dismiss them. Later, in a similar way, I began to filter out the statistics chatter about Christianity moving south, about a global church in the South, in order to see better what local and specific forms authentic Christianity was actually taking. That matters more than the numbers.

The Fear Factor

In November 1979, when President Reagan's anti-Communist belligerence and election victory resulted in renewed Cold War suspicions, several members of the MCC executive board, who had been in Germany for an inter-Mennonite consultation on the future of MCC work in Europe, traveled with me through the corridor to Berlin. We passed through a checkpoint in the Berlin wall in order to participate in a seminar with Gossner Mission pastors and theologians in East Berlin. On our way back, once through Checkpoint Charlie and back on the Ubahn train, those leaders began to relax, and laugh at jokes in a near giddy fashion, as if we were going home from a bar. A bit later, when that board debated at length, then approved a continued East–West program that included placing persons in East Germany among other things, Peter Dyck sent me a tape recording of the debate and decision moment. What struck me was the nervous laughter once again, as if we were going to stick our finger in the Soviet nose, were doing something daring that parts of the constituency would worry about. I had always avoided using the phrase Iron Curtain, or Iron Curtain countries, but after listening to the tittering, I began wondering which side was really behind the Iron Curtain. Over the past two decades, the conviction has grown that although the East took down not only the Berlin wall, but also other forms of Iron Curtain separation, I have been living and teaching in a country still imprisoned in fear behind the Iron Curtain. Is such fear a good thing for Americans, or at least for Christian Americans, who, one would think, were trusting in God? Can we learn to love the "enemy" from a position of fear?

This calls to mind personal moments of anxiety and fear, a chain of experiences that caused me to have more sympathy with Soviet and East European border officials who thought I was dangerous. On my first extended stay in the USSR (1973), among my first tasks was to locate and visit places of Christian worship, especially the evangelical Christian Baptist congregations that were often on the outskirts. No information service could or would give me the address or telephone number. After the service at the good-sized congregation in Leningrad, several younger persons walked me back to the bus stop. Not long after, I noticed the usual raincoat and hat type following me at a distance. In Moscow at the Baptist headquarters, the Mennonite staff member, Viktor Kriger, quickly told me with his eyes that there were ears (or recording devices) behind the curtains, and proposed that we go for a walk in the crisp sunshine. Even then, we switched to Low German dialect, and kept a lookout as we talked. Many years later I stumbled upon official reports (in state archives) to the authorities about such foreign visitors. I published one of them as part of a similar event from 1980 that reported a Mennonite World Conference visit to Alma-Ata (now Almaty), Kazakhstan, of Paul Kraybill, the general secretary, and Walter Sawatsky as the specialist. The closing lines of that report, sent from the official in Kazakhstan to Moscow, were to advise them to limit the influence of Sawatsky because he was encouraging the young people in their religious activities. As some may know, I became *de facto persona non grata* for seven long years, reduced to making contacts with Baptist leaders via a proxy or by meeting them at events in the West.[9]

I noticed two things through these experiences. My background knowledge told me that the state persecution had deeply frightened older leaders who returned from prison rather cowed, whereas a newer generation was accustomed to the setting, and tended to think that if one activity was forbidden, what were alternative options to explore. They were much less shaped by fear, rather by hope.

On that Kazakhstan trip, Jakob Doerksen from Kyrgyzstan told me things even the files later discovered by Johannes Dyck did not convey. A week or so before my letter to Mennonite and Baptist leaders in Kyrgyzstan reached them, informing them of our visit to Alma-Ata and our hope that they might meet us, the KGB had called Doerksen in to say that he was forbidden to go to the meeting with Sawatsky in Alma-Ata. Doerksen said he knew nothing about it, but managed to elicit enough data to know the precise dates, and declared that there was no law against visiting friends in Kazakhstan. To play safe, he had slipped out of his workplace by a rear door, took the car he had hidden nearby, and drove all night to see me at the hotel the next morning. When he returned home, the authorities again interrogated him for eight hours. This he told me some years later when he had immigrated to Germany, and came to visit at our home. I apologized for the trouble I had caused him, but he waved it away, saying that the opportunity for fellowship with Mennonites from abroad

---

9 See Walter Sawatsky, "Glimpses Behind the Curtain — Surveillance and Pressure during Church Delegation Visits," *Religion in Eastern Europe* 32, no. 4 (November 2012): 41–46.

was worth it.

So what reason did I have to fear the authorities, who could easily keep me for interrogation, or confiscate my papers (as happened several times), but then my foreign passport guaranteed my relative security? Reflecting on those Soviet times now, I am saddened, because of my painful awareness that those same 50,000 or more Soviet Mennonite Evangelicals — who at great personal risk had kept seeking fellowship with the global Mennonite world — after having immigrated to Germany in the early 1990s — refused to join the Mennonite World Conference (MWC) because it seemed alien; they no longer trusted its leadership. It tells us that the careful balancing between left- and right-wing sentiments in our Mennonite worlds, too easily swayed by current American culture wars, is not working well enough. We need a greater capacity for seeing from their point of view. We need a greater capacity to stop assuming that we in America own and define what makes one Mennonite and Christian, before global church relations can go deeper.

The 1989 Surprise?

A year or so before my visa to go to the USSR (January 1988) finally came through, I was watching television coverage of Pope John Paul II's second visit to Poland. I marveled less at the reality of the trip, or at the Pope's speeches to the youth, than at the journalists who still lacked the vocabulary and religious imagination to make sense of what was happening. Hence "everyone" was surprised when the nonviolent revolutions of 1989 came about. To see it actually happening, to experience the euphoria of reunifications in Germany, or the peaceful ending of the attempted coup in Moscow when the women talked the soldiers into refusing to shoot on the people, were indeed times for deep emotion, for saying this is unbelievable, or even that there must be an angel somewhere. But to careful observers and participants, the changes were happening long before already.

Another moment of surprise for me, instead, was to do a presentation to the Mennonite Historical Society in Goshen in 1986, where I described the developments since the crushing of Solidarity in 1981, using Jonathan Schell's references to the "politics of decency" in Czechoslovakia and Poland, and to realize that my listeners were responding in disbelief. They might have been teaching the way of pacifism, but at some deep level had accepted the greater realism of nuclear power — they could not imagine how its actual use had become impotent as an instrument of foreign policy. Since those days, I have wished for more careful attention to political, social, and cultural developments around the world, and less deference to the peaceful and democratic claims of the American Government, and more attention to the actual policies of repression, and now outright torture of our government. We have remained largely quiescent along with the majority of our society.

So a major turning point for me has been our former reliance on the global cultural framework of human rights expectations, that once gave Amnesty International and Human Rights Watch their journalistic clout and negotiating capacity, but our country's need for security against an announced terror threat (which is different from an actual threat commensurate with the kinds of state response to "global terrorism") has us deferring to our people's fears. The violation of rights argument has been blunted; how can we as Americans raise it in an appeal to do the decent thing, to stop the torture and release the political and religious prisoners, when the perpetrators are us? Indeed, it is difficult to recall when Mennonite mission leaders focused consultation time on the problem of doing authentic mission when we are so deeply associated with America's global dominance.

Elusive Road to Mutuality

One day as I was speaking in a group discussion session at a Church and Peace conference in Germany, I heard myself contrasting the peace churches with the war churches. No one corrected me, presumably out of courtesy, but I have no memory of the rest of that conversation. How could I be so arrogant to claim the high road for the "peace churches" (knowing how poorly we have lived that peace witness) and suggest the others were the war churches? Does any Christian tradition truly see a mandate to make war and its requisite killing of enemies, whenever lectionary reading of Romans 12 or Matthew 5 comes around? Soon after I was invited to speak about Mennonite peacemaking experiences to a north German association of Protestant clergy, only to discover in the coffee time that the majority of those present were pacifists because of their reading of the New Testament, possibly shaped by Bonhoeffers's writings, or those of Martin Niemoeller. They might be the only peace Christian in their parish, and had to tread circumspectly, but people noticed how their convictions showed in the local initiatives they fostered and they signaled their appreciation.

It reminded me of my first encounter with Hans Adolf Hertzler, of Krefeld, pastor of the then largest Mennonite church in Germany, with a membership of a thousand, even though on an average Sunday only forty or fifty were present. I knew of Hertzler as a scholar with a doctorate in Anabaptist studies. He stated that in light of the two previous pastors, each with forty years of ministry — one a Lutheran with Lutheran two kingdoms theology, and the other a Lutheran theologically — he had given himself twenty-five years to work toward the goal of once again becoming a peace church, that Krefeld church which in 1683 had sent its first immigrants to USA in order to avoid military service. I got to watch him work over the next few years, noticed how carefully he listened, how seldom he spoke but how he encouraged others to do so. Although since then I have been in the USA for nearly thirty years, I keep noticing what comes out of that Krefeld church through its members. So what makes a church a peace church? Talking a good line is seldom more than a superficial answer.

Since 1978 I have been attending the annual meetings of the Council of International Ministries (CIM), a gathering of mission and MCC program executives from at least thirteen Mennonite denominations. At times we managed to host delegates from Latin America, or from Europe, and at the Mennonite World assemblies since 1978 there has usually been a prefatory gathering of mission representatives from around the world. At such a preparatory meeting in 1975 in San Juan, Puerto Rico, there was much talk about deepening partnerships around the world. It was the time when various mission societies — such as the Latin American Mission, or the Church Missionary Society, or the United Bible Societies — experimented with more globally mutual forms of decision making and financing. So the code word thereafter has been "mutuality" in mission. At subsequent CIM gatherings Bob Ramseyer, as director of AMBS's Mission Training Center, presented papers seeking to spell out what mutuality in mission could mean, how to restructure ourselves toward it. I recall my own enthusiasm for working in that direction, since the MCC style still was to see itself as working on behalf of all Mennonites and related bodies, including some of the Amish, and not needing to dominate and polish its image, but to give visibility to the smaller church entities. I say still was, because by the time of the New Wineskins review process after about 2002, it seemed as if key staff and board members were not acquainted with that history. That is a quick way of saying how many complicating factors can arise as staff transitions take place, or board members get elected who came with good will and no background.

The CIM process of regional program reviews and general meetings to keep abreast of some of the trends in missiological thinking was somewhat effective as an accountability body.[10] By 2000 however, the level of constituency support

---

10 In two pamphlet-length articles, Wilbert Shenk provided a historical review, including key documents: *An Experiment in Interagency Cooperation* (Elkhart, IN: Council of International Ministries, 1986); *God's New Economy: Interdependence and Mission* (Elkhart, IN: Mission Focus Pamphlet, 1988). More recent articles in *Mission Focus* addressed some later developments in inter-Mennonite mission cooperation; but given my own participation, I still sense an obligation to attempt a review and assessment through at least 2012.

for mission and MCC programs had been on a steady decline, evident in both a drop in long-term personnel and funding, and a shift to greater reliance on big donors and foundations. Several of us wrote papers around 2000 on what seemed a more elusive road to mutuality in ministry and mission, which taught me about new pitfalls. One way toward mutuality that was broadly voiced was to strengthen Mennonite World Conference (MWC) as an instrument for shared exercise of churchly power. Financial and idea power surely needed to be less heavily North American, and secondly European; nevertheless we found no transition device to make it happen. Over the space of three years initially, the CIM members authorized its representatives at MWC gatherings to support the formation of a global mission forum, hopefully with decision making and funding powers. Looking at what has developed in the past decade, what strikes me as a social historian is to observe the many ways apparent mutuality is manipulated from behind the scenes, mostly out of good will. But too many of the able leaders from the "South," with large member churches, live in settings of great financial stringency, and there are still limits to sufficient talented leaders, so that naming such leaders to world Mennonite roles not only weakens the work at home. It also sets up such leaders for discouragement since they lack the communication tools and skills that those from better endowed churches take for granted. This past decade has also been a time of intensified pressures from supporting churches and their board members in North America to do program assessments, usually for reasons arising not from good missiological principles, but from donor satisfaction needs. That does not bode well for long-term North American engagement in global mission.

The Instruments of Ministry

Throughout my time as seminary teacher, I found myself returning regularly to the question — what is good teaching, in fact, what must we teach, and what methods make for effective teaching? The best I can report is how rare were the moments when intended teaching happened, less rare when people indicated they had learned, and I wondered about the teacher's role in that. Indeed, to replace teacher with preacher or pastor could well lead to very similar conclusions. There is a reciprocity to teaching, and a mysterious serendipity when capacity to teach something and capacity to receive and learn come together. So what has been most consistent for me is the realization, at the end of most terms, that teaching the class had made it possible for me to change my mind, to have some more "aha" moments. So I keep hoping that as I work at the "to do list" still left, I will keep on learning to see and think better, and to contribute something to living globally.

Most of the instruments of ministry that I relied on were idea-related: researching, interviewing, fostering archival collections or using them, planning and review meetings, writing memos or letters of encouragement or counsel, and often conversing in multilinguistic and multi-confessional settings. How does one measure these, except to do what you know to be right? Our East–West presence ministry was very small: one or two persons as students or teachers in a country, learning the language and engaging professors and students. So we planned retreats of our EastWest Fraternity for a particular country, where the MCC personnel could use the occasion to invite someone to lecture to us and engage in conversation, or we made a presentation to a group of local friends, which became a reference point to build on in relationship building, having conveyed that this is a church-based, not merely individual relationship building effort across the East–West divide. Once we met with a newly established Mennonite fellowship in Budapest — heady stuff, but it did not last, which also set us to pondering.

The apostle Paul's note to his colleague to bring the books and the parchments often served as a reminder about the importance of book missionaries. Together with Mennonite Broadcasts we coordinated translations into local languages of some of the Mennonite Faith pamphlets. A bigger editing and coordinating project was the Barclay Commentary translation project. That story has been told in print several ways. What is worth recalling is how many times along the way, as the Cold War ebbed and flowed or the likelihood of getting an official license to import and distribute copies seemed more doubtful, both MCC boards and Baptist World Alliance boards debated and challenged themselves to trust that a way would open, that the money we raised and spent was not a waste. Permission finally came through; a magic moment to notice how a project, which we did openly and many knew about, so quickly got owned as our shared project across the East–West divide.

When I returned to editing journals during the last sixteen years of my time at AMBS, it too was a tool of ministry, a way, especially with the new internet access and email deliveries, to facilitate thinking persons' writing about theology, mission, peace, or the task of rebuilding a good civil society across Eurasia, to talk with each other, who were unable to do so face-to-face.

But there were moments I thought about long after. Once Alan Krieder, who was very active in the early 1980s peace movement in Britain, as some of us were on the European continent, invited me to give a speech at a gathering in London. Present were mostly evangelical Anglicans, Methodists, Baptists, and persons from related societies, such as Frances Schaeffer's L'Abri movement. The speakers presented just war, pacifist, and a kind of necessary war involvement, given our fallen world, ways of thinking. My assignment was to speak about praxis from my East European experience.

I remember telling one story about an occasion when, in the Baptist church of Minsk, just before the last major sermon was to be preached, the door opened and in walked the head of the state religious affairs office for that region. The quick-thinking pastor welcomed the visitor, then indicated they would have a time of spoken prayers, before the last sermon. There was the usual murmur of voices, until one woman's prayer grew louder and others listened as she thanked God for their many blessings. She thanked God for the freedom of worship they were enjoying, for food to eat, for law and order in the city, for its officials who tried to do their work honestly when that was not so easy. Then she went on to pray for divine blessing on General Secretary Leonid Brezhnev, the leader of the Soviet Union. Help him, in spite of the many challenges, to push for the way of peace in the world, so we would never again experience the killing and suffering of the Great Fatherland war, when everyone there had lost a loved one. It was a story illustrating ways of doing what you can, and praying for friend and enemy was an obvious one. To my surprise, the session chair, a retired admiral, remarked that he had never thought of prayer in that way, as praying that God would bless the enemy, but why would the lady not pray for her government, even if it was regularly harassing their church life, because the Bible told us to do so? Too many things we fail to think of, until something causes you to notice.

I had encountered an officer at that gathering, then on the Prime Minister's advisory board for nuclear preparedness, but an evangelical Christian, who had earlier confessed his aloneness because his work was so highly confidential. So how was he to find his way as responsible Christian? When it came time to join together in communion, I chose to share the cup with him as an act of fraternal solidarity, although we knew we were on quite opposite sides of peace/war theological positions, but before our Lord and Savior, we stood as sinners saved by grace.

So often when I was in settings where there was surveillance, especially in Soviet days or elsewhere in Eastern Europe, it seemed prudent to censor one's speech. When Helmut Doerksen and I traveled to visit churches in Hungary, Czechoslovakia, Romania, and Yugoslavia, we kept noticing that the pastors or sometimes bishops we met indicated they could not trust their colleagues. So we began thinking of ourselves as de facto visiting bishops, to whom they could pour out their thoughts and feelings, allowing them to try out thought options for how to proceed, and promising them confidentiality. Sometimes I wrote up a confidential report, but often those were pretty general in tone. Nevertheless, the more we thought about it, the more we sensed that an important instrument of ministry we should risk was to seek to speak openly. We were not going to be like the Navigator missionary I once encountered in Poland, with whom I went for a long walk since it was obvious we were both believers, but only after two hours did he acknowledge (I guess because I knew his agency style already) that he was not a business person really, but a missionary of the Navigators, providing teaching materials for Catholic youth camps.

Sitting in our hotel room late one night after an all-day visit to the Baptist Union congress in Moscow, and unwinding, Peter Dyck and I decided we would speak freely to the hidden microphones. A half hour later, the listeners had learned a great deal about what was happening within the General Conference Mennonite church in USA, how we should seek to resolve an issue, and we hoped that might give them a better education than for them to keep listening for when we might drop the name of some local Mennonite leaders, who could then be accused of telling secrets to foreign church leaders. At least for us, we recognized it as a liberating act, even in our private moments we had felt free to state our deep love for God's church, in spite of its problems, and that was also how we talked with believers in the open parks the next afternoon.

The world is still very local, and the languages of faith are very many, so the road to living globally in God's church remains very difficult. Also daunting is the decline of Christianity in comparison to other religions, and especially to the growth and persistence of peoples living as if there is no God, as if the moral order of justice and peace for all no longer applies as shared human vision. So I close at this point with the reminder made by many, and so often spoken with despair, that we start to lose a meaningful sense that God so loved the world when we forget about each other, when we no longer bother to learn and remember the larger story, the evangel for all.

Book Reviews

Colin Godwin, *Baptizing, Gathering, and Sending: Anabaptist Mission in the Sixteenth-Century Context*, Pandora Press, Kitchener, Ontario, Canada, 2012. 422 pp. $32.99 (CAD). ISBN: 9781926599250.

Baptizing, Gathering, and Sending is an exploration of the missionary practices and beliefs of Anabaptist founders with the aim of stirring contemporary Anabaptists to a historically informed mission. Author Colin Godwin carefully narrates the social and religious climate of the sixteenth century in which the Anabaptist movement was birthed, wades through primary resources, and offers contemporary application and reflection for our crumbling Christendom context.

To explicate the missiology of early Anabaptist leaders — among whom are usual suspects, like Hans Hut, Pilgram Marpeck, and Conrad Grebel, but also lesser knowns, like David Joris — Godwin employs the Missio Dei (the mission of God) as his interpretive lens. This methodology — which sees "the triune God [as] the initiator of divine mission to lovingly draw men and women into his Kingdom" — is the foundation of his engagement. Godwin explains that this emphasis sets this study apart from previous efforts (31). Up until the Second World War — the last time, Godwin claims, that a significant analysis of this kind was done — the dominant interpretation was based on the presence or absence of evangelistic missions beyond Christendom. The results have not been positive. Most have cast the sixteenth-century Anabaptists as un-missionary, thus neglecting their missionary efforts (at deep cost) in local contexts: "Religious protagonists of the era were not obliged to send missionaries across the seas in order to find a person in need of conversion: such people were living on their doorsteps in every corner of Europe" (33).

Godwin counters by offering an account of Anabaptism as a movement which created communities of "minority witness" (192). He identifies how the act of baptism was not merely focused on conversion. It was also an act of entrance, an act in which a person chose to participate, an act which constituted a welcoming and dynamic community, an act that set the baptized apart from other communities:

> Believers' baptism for the Anabaptists was the cornerstone of the creation of a new kind of church, a believing community bound by Christ's moral imperatives, prepared to live in alternative community amidst the corruption and decay the Anabaptists found around them. They were, after all, called re-baptizers, not re-converters. Baptism was central to both their missionary practice and ecclesial identity. (135)

As I reflect on my experience of church and my work as a youth pastor, it's easy to see how this discussion offers some challenges. In a few weeks, I will baptize a few friends in our community. Do we really understand the depth of this practice? How radical it is or, at least, how radical our tradition once believed it to be? Can we grasp the ways that it might animate our church as a people sent into and for the world, sent into our neighborhoods?

Yet it is Godwin's discussion of Anabaptism as "minority witness" that strikes home even more. How can we, in our First World, 'post-Christian' realities (I write from Canada), learn from the marginal witness of our sixteenth-century elders? Godwin argues that current Anabaptist understandings around 'post-Christendom' are too superficial. It's not:

> simply about the loss of status of the churches in the West but the loss of status of the West period. The growth of the church in Asia, Africa, and South America anticipated by Visser 't Hooft in 1959, became a reality that none could ignore by the end of the twentieth century and shows no signs of slowing in the twenty-first. (293)

How should we respond? According to Godwin, to be an Anabaptist witness, especially in the First World, demands that we have a global perspective in each of our local contexts. Since many white Anabaptists in the West find themselves in positions of power, I believe that we must learn from marginalized voices that have been overwhelmingly silenced, directly or not, by white power. Anabaptism cannot be a minority witness — and thus true to its tradition, and more importantly, true to the gospel — unless it sheds its reliance and trust in the vestiges of Christendom and Western power.

As we struggle to live and practice Anabaptism today, it is important that we understand the foundations which animated the movement at the beginning. It's important for us to track how those foundations have been re-imagined over the centuries and explore how we might do the same in our particular time and place. Godwin's book is not perfect — it's a bit too academic to garner a wide reading — but it contains valuable resources that can help us do this vital work of "seeking the old paths" (Jer. 6:16).

CHRIS LENSHYN, *Associate Pastor at Emmanuel Mennonite Church, Abbotsford, British Columbia, Canada.*

John Howard Yoder, *Theology of Mission: A Believers Church Perspective,* **edited by Gayle Gerber Koontz and Andy Alexis-Baker, IVP Academic, Downers Grove, IL, 2014. 430 pp. $36.00. ISBN: 9780830840335.**

Between 1964 and 1983, John Howard Yoder taught a course on the theology of mission at Associated Mennonite Biblical Seminaries. After Yoder left the seminary the tapes were stored in the library basement and forgotten. Decades later, while guest lecturing in Gayle Gerber Koontz's course on the theological legacy of Yoder, Wilber Shenk alluded to the possibility that the tapes of Yoder's lectures might still exist, and after months of searching they were found. This book is the culmination of transcribing and editing the audio recordings of Yoder's course from 1973 and 1976. The result of this fascinating and laborious process is a major contribution to the present work of understanding the church's mission.

While the book is not formally divided, the chapters move broadly through biblical, historical, and theological engagements. Chapters 1 through 5 deal with the Bible, offering Yoder's attentive reading of Scripture which attempts to bracket later histories of interpretation. In the Bible, Yoder finds an account in which people are called, brought into covenant relationship, and expected to live as a *particular people* in light of that calling. In the Old Testament this is primarily through the election of Israel in the midst of the nations. In the Gospels, the call remains the same - be faithful as Israel was called to be faithful. In the book of Acts, as well as in the Pauline corpus, a shift takes place; here there is reflection on what happened in the spread of this movement, not an articulation of a strategic plan. "The fact of mission," Yoder asserts, "was prior to the theology of mission" (96). Later, in summarizing his exegetical work on the New Testament, Yoder writes, "[The mission] was unavoidable and even sometimes accidental. The Diaspora base was in place before the Gospel. In this sense the 'new people' *was* the message before it became the vehicle for the message" (124). This reading becomes an important orientation for Yoder. Throughout the text, he unpacks and sets forth a mission of *migration*. This mission reflects an existing community that, through its particular calling, moves and engages the world around it.

After establishing his reading of the biblical material, Yoder situates this narrative within the history of mission (and its theology) and then grapples more directly with contemporary theological issues. In the sections on the history of mission, readers familiar with Yoder will find the usual critique of Constantinianism and its perversion of the message of the gospel. While this critique is increasingly familiar, the historical and theological terrain Yoder covers with regard to mission provides a fresh perspective on his engagement, especially with his extended dialogue (and critique) of Pietism.

Chapter 15 marks a transition into more contemporary theological territory. Yoder explains the Free Church approach as one uninterested in large social engineering in the name of salvation. Rather, it is a movement that provides internal social critique which varies with given situations. The gospel still speaks in its radical particularity, and the message comes via the presence of a people committed to loving service. The mission is, in one sense, quite simple: ongoing engagement with the message of the gospel as it relates to specific environments.

Working towards something of a climax, Yoder approaches the basic questions of Christianity's relation to other religions. Until now, Yoder has outlined an image of the church in mission that needed to repent of and reject past complicity with colonial projects. However, it remains an open question as to whether Yoder actually addresses the underlying logic that led to the destructive elements of the church's mission. He makes two claims in these final chapters that will need to be acknowledged and engaged by future theologians in this field. First, while discussing 'religion' as an interpretive category, Yoder asserts that "what Christians must talk about is Jesus Christ, not Christianity as religion or culture" (397). This position is compounded with a second claim, having to do with the way in which Jesus 'positions' other religions and post-Christian movements. Yoder does not advocate active proselytizing of Hindus and Buddhists but articulates how *they are changed* when they come into contact with Jesus. Then with respect to post-Christian movements (anything from Islam to Marxism), Yoder contends that they are "derived from a Christianity that lost its way" (385). I'm suspicious of Yoder's way of explaining the relationship between Christianity and other religious movements because he makes it sound like there is some pure *essence* of truth within the Christian tradition that remains unassailable in the face of colonial experiences and wrongdoing. For Yoder, the essence, which cannot be wrong, is Jesus. But does that not contradict his emphasis on the particularity of Jesus? I don't think it is helpful to both prioritize Jesus's particularity *and* abstract some essence which remains an unassailable element of the Christian tradition.

Theology of Mission is an important contribution to what is at present a controversial topic. Yoder calls on the church to live out of its particular history and formation. This means confessing the wrongs that came from it and returning again and again to the biblical witness, which points the church towards a communal and migratory understanding of mission. These are welcome correctives to many supercessionist theologies of mission. The question that remains untouched is whether Yoder actually steers the church away from a theology that will insulate itself from *receiving* good news outside of (and perhaps otherwise than) its particularity — a theology of mission that cannot help but determine the question of salvation for others. Such a theology, weighted more on repentance than a reflexive posture of mutual engagement and formation, also adds to the tension the Mennonite church faces as it continues to sort out not only its understanding of mission but also its handling of the accounts of Yoder's sexual abuse. The Mennonite Church is currently not of one mind on these issues, but this work should stand as an important contribution to these ongoing conversations.

DAVID DRIEDGER, *Associate Minister at First Mennonite Church, Winnipeg, Manitoba, Canada.*

J. Denny Weaver, *The Nonviolent God,* Eerdmans, Grand Rapids, MI, 2013. 336 pp. $25.00. ISBN: 9780802869234.

I am nearing the end of my three-year commitment with Christian Peacemaker Teams (CPT) and I plan to renew as a reservist, because I want to deepen my exploration of the "radicality of God's justice" (21), a way of life described by J. Denny Weaver in his theologically rich book, The Nonviolent God.

Readers familiar with CPT and its work of violence reduction (work that Weaver has participated in and references within this text) will know that we embrace non-violence and a theological vision that is marginal to mainstream Christianity. So, Weaver was preaching his text to the choir (albeit, a critical one). I'm on board with his rejection of divine violence. I agree with his privileging of interpretations of the gospel that come from the underside of society. And, above all, I agree with how he centres everything on the praxis of the nonviolent Christ who was crucified – a focus that produces "a theology for the living."

God is present in the life of Jesus. Through Jesus' embodied witness of the Kingdom, God engaged the brokenness of our fragile world: the outcasts and suspects, the ethnically despised and reviled. But it wasn't only interpersonal relationships that God addressed in Jesus. It was also those larger systemic forces that impacted — often disastrously so — relationships in and between communities.

God unmasked the powers and gave life in Jesus. Yet it's not all about Jesus. It's also about you and me and the entire creation. Because God raised the Crucified who embodied a truly human way of being, writes Weaver, the resurrection "is an invitation to every individual to experience reconciliation with God and the presence of the reign of God now on earth, in our lives as human beings" (87). This demands decision — personal and collective. "Experiencing the reign of God now requires a choice on our part to leave the forces of evil and to join the reign of God made present in the life of the resurrected Jesus" (87). Sadly, as we are all too aware, the church has largely strayed from the blueprint which is to guide our seeking of God's reign — that is, the very life of Jesus. Weaver explicates this failure in some detail.

It didn't take long before the church was woven into the mainstream fabric of the Roman Empire. Forgetting its history and the subversive gospel memories, the Christian community lost its sense of confrontation with the dominant social order. One memory that challenged such amnesia was the New Testament book of Revelation.

The book of Revelation is not a predictive text about some distant, future calamity. Revelation was and is a warning about complacency in the present. Specifically, Revelation implores first-century readers not to become comfortable or deceived by an empire that is not actively oppressing Christians. At the time, Rome was not persecuting the church. Christians were tolerated and largely ignored. And it was during this period, and the following decades, that a new Christian identity was emerging; one that focused on the relationship between God the Father and the Son as deity. Regrettably, what this Son actually did while physically present on Earth — his radical kingdom ministry of non-violent resistance — was being eclipsed by a high Christology which privileged Jesus' divinity. According to Weaver, the book of Revelation is a bold call to remember that the one on the throne is the Crucified who confronted the domination system, and was slaughtered for doing it.

It is a word that is desperately needed today. Whether we identify the empire as the United States, or perhaps even global capital (as Weaver does), how do we move from complacency to resistance? And, coming to the crux of the book, how do we do it non-violently?

Weaver defines violence as "destruction to a victim by means that overpower the victim's consent" (192). We need thicker and more complex definitions than this. For in this imperial age of ecological plunder, inordinate harm is done to other-than-human persons that aren't able to articulate consent. Can we recognize that? Can we define violence as a power that dominates, destroys, and diminishes not only ourselves but all of creation (and so define non-violence as a power that liberates and heals human and non-human creation)? Such understandings would fit nicely within Weaver's "theology for the living."

Weaver also falls short in addressing North American economic realities. He states that Jesus did not propose a specific economic system but rather an order that promoted financial, environmental, and social sustainability. But then he curiously states that, as Christians, our calling is not to join efforts to replace one system with another (i.e., capitalist to socialist), but to use available mechanisms within the system to advocate for the marginalized. While giving detailed examples of what this could look like — examples which address the recent financial collapse and current health crisis within the United States — Weaver's reliance on the profit system is problematic. Capitalism certainly does not liberate, humanize, and heal ourselves and the rest of creation. And I don't think Jesus would be comfortable with the idea of working towards a kinder, gentler form of this system. As a Christian, I hear the words of Jesus ("Woe to the rich," "Blessed be the poor," for example) and the vision of the book of Revelation as calling all of us — whether you are an Indigenous Native American or a wealthy white Zacchaeus — to join a revolution. The invitation of the crucified and resurrected Jesus is to experience and practice the reign of God, now, on Earth. That is the good news of the non-violent God.

CHRIS SABAS, *Christian Peacemaker Teams – Aboriginal Justice Team, Toronto, Ontario, Canada.*

Willard M. Swartley, *Health, Healing and the Church's Mission: Biblical Perspectives and Moral Priorities*, IVP Academic, Downers Grove, IL, 2012. 268 pp. $19.20. ISBN: 9780830839742.

As I began reading this book, there was an outbreak of measles in the Fraser Valley where I live. Measles is a highly contagious viral infection and a potentially serious disease, but in communities with high vaccination rates, it's generally not a problem. In fact, fifteen years ago, the immunization program was so successful that people spoke of measles being eliminated in North America.

In the eastern part of the Fraser Valley, however, the vaccination rate was only 60–70%, well below the 95% needed for effective immunity in a community. Several children had confirmed diagnoses, there were another hundred suspected cases all at the same religious school, and the infection was beginning to spread beyond the school to the general population.

One of the reasons for the low vaccination rate in that particular area is the belief that, if it is God's will, God will protect people from disease. "We leave it in [God's] hands," says the pastor of the church at the center of the outbreak. While he does not oppose healthy eating, rest, and other natural ways of staying healthy, he is against vaccination. "Of course I openly express my own point of view according to the Bible, absolutely," he says. "But it's not that we force [people not to vaccinate]. It's through their own conscience that they have to act."

It would seem that this pastor's teaching has had an effect, for vaccination rates in his community are relatively low compared to that of surrounding areas, and they were now facing this outbreak of measles. Was this really God's will? Or does God will us to use medicine and science to prevent disease? What does it mean for God to be our healer? And what role does the community play in health and healing?

Willard Swartley's book is a comprehensive treatment of these and other questions. I appreciate his careful biblical scholarship in Part 1 of the text, which gives an overview of healing in both the Old and New Testaments, offers sound theological analysis, and discusses the church as a community of healing. In Part 2, Swartley thoughtfully applies this understanding to current issues of health care in the United States, and extends this even further in Part 3 as he explores new paradigms of compassionate and sustainable health care that express mutual aid, service, and God's shalom.

Swartley's purpose in writing this book is to recall the church "to own its biblical, historical and theological heritage and its mission in healing and health care. It challenges the current dominant assumption that health care is an economic, political or medical issue only. It regards U.S. health care a moral priority" (11).

To the pastor who sees vaccination as a lack of faith, this book says: "We should not pit faith healing against medical healing. We need not compartmentalize between the religious and the scientific, between natural and supernatural healing, between faith and pills" (100). "Medical cures rooted in scientific knowledge do not negate God as healer who gives wholeness and well-being" (107).

For the church seeking to live out its mission, this book reminds us of "Jesus' dual mission of healing and proclaiming the kingdom of God" (11). It calls us "to continue what Jesus began: to be a healing community" (17), and reminds us that "The quality of the church's life and mission is known by its response to the weak, the disabled and the poor in its midst" (163).

For those who are sick, there is both realism and hope that comes both from Scripture and from the author's own experience with his heart condition: "Healing is always God's/Jesus' gift; it is not *our* faith or doing. And when we are not healed from physical sickness as we might desire, we may experience other dimensions of healing, emotional and spiritual, and know shalom-joy even when health is compromised" (229).

For those in our culture who tend to idolize health and the perfect body, this book reminds us of our all too human limitations, "to own our mortality and open ourselves to God's work in and through us" (44), to see the "beauty and grace" in disability (166).

For healthcare leaders and others, this book sets out a vision of health care that "honors God's good creation" (207), that is compassionate and just, and cares for those who are most vulnerable.

While the healthcare system and its challenges are somewhat different in Canada than in the United States, I resonated with so much in this book and found myself underlining these and many other passages. I highly recommend this biblical, practical, wise, and challenging book.

As for the measles outbreak in my neighboring community? The 320 confirmed cases is the largest measles outbreak ever recorded in my province. A medical health spokesperson expressed respect for the group's religious views and at the same time encouraged others to get vaccinated. Extra clinics were set up for vaccination and were used by the general population and some members of the religious group who decided to get vaccinated as well. The outbreak was largely limited to the one area, and the crisis seems to be over.

APRIL YAMASAKI, *Pastor of Emmanuel Mennonite Church, Abbotsford, British Columbia, Canada.*

Mark R. Amstutz, *Evangelicals and American Foreign Policy*, Oxford University Press, 2014. 260 pp. $29.95. ISBN: 9780199987634.

In *Evangelicals and American Foreign Policy* Mark Amstutz provides an overview of the ways in which evangelicals in the United States have been involved in foreign affairs as well as a normative account for how their work in this area might be strengthened. The paradigm highlighted (and generally praised) throughout the book is that of neo-evangelicalism: a movement of theologically conservative Protestants who rejected fundamentalist isolationism in the mid-twentieth century in order to engage with politics and culture. In Amstutz's view, neo-evangelicals (such as Carl F. H. Henry, the magazine *Christianity Today*, and the National Association of Evangelicals, or NAE) represent a brand of faith in line with historical evangelicalism's nineteenth-century efforts to minister to broader society. In regards to the historical roots of their foreign affairs engagement, Amstutz identifies overseas missions as the original mode by which evangelicals began to influence geopolitical conversations. Foreign missionaries were "the first American internationalists" (66) who laid the foundation for Christian and secular conceptions of global humanitarianism and civil society.

Several chapters of the book deal with specific foreign policy issues of particular significance to US evangelicals, such as global poverty, Israel, immigration, and the war on terror. Amstutz registers several praises and concerns with the manner in which evangelicals engaged these issues. For example, he salutes evangelicals for their important role in the push for US assistance in the HIV/AIDS pandemic in Africa but criticizes what he sees as a naïve sense of empathy for undocumented immigrants and terrorist detainees among some evangelicals. The criticisms largely fall at the feet of more progressive evangelical thinkers (such as Ron Sider and David Gushee) and the more recent public statements made by the NAE, all of which are, according to Amstutz, unwilling to enter into the difficult work of balancing compassionate concerns with the complications of statecraft. Evangelicals must not ignore the demands of the rule of law upon illegal aliens and the financial burden they place on the US (180–1), or the fact that "limited coercive interrogation" of terrorists may be justified when community safety is threatened (186).

In the final chapter of the book, "Toward a More Effective Evangelical Global Engagement," Amstutz articulates an international vision for evangelicals that balances competing claims of justice and humanitarianism, and the broader tension between worldly engagement with what he sees as the primarily spiritual task of the church. Drawing upon sources such as neo-evangelical Carl F. H. Henry and Christian realist Reinhold Niebuhr, he calls on evangelicals to engage in international politics through identification of general moral principles but to reject the temptation (that Amstutz identifies as the pitfall of the Protestant mainline) to "tell the government what to do" (199). Quoting Paul Ramsey, Amstutz contends that "in politics the church is only a theoretician" and that blunt statements (such as the NAE's on torture) "call into question the moral authority of the church itself because these political initiatives were often regarded as simplistic, divisive, and unrepresentative of their member's views" (199).

A strength of this book is its historical account of evangelical influence in US foreign policy, particularly its linkage of the development of US geopolitics with the Christian missionary enterprise. For those interested in missions, Amstutz helpfully reminds us that Christian work abroad can never be understood without political dynamics in mind. Missionaries (even those of Anabaptist persuasion) must be aware of the ways in which they represent (often unconsciously) their homeland's cultural and political interests on the international scene, for better or worse. Likewise, those concerned primarily with foreign policy must come to terms with the fact that their enterprise has never been a purely secular matter. Missionaries were historically instrumental in developing the global consciousness of Americans and have been an important lobbying influence in US foreign policy.

Though most Anabaptists (and some evangelicals) will disagree with the more pious version of a Christian realist political theology that Amstutz proffers, his views are worth consideration if for no other reason than their ubiquity among the culturally competent and politically astute evangelicals that have taken up residence in the halls of U.S. power in the last half-century. Theological differences aside though, a weakness in the method and scope of this book is that Amstutz focuses most of his criticism of evangelical geopolitical work on progressive evangelical figureheads and the formal statements of evangelical groups, while neglecting close analysis of the actual beliefs and profound influence of the more typically conservative evangelical laity. This is most glaring in his discussions of evangelical views on immigration, nuclear war, and torture (his more nuanced discussion of the varieties of evangelical support for Israel being the exception). I wish Amstutz would have spent more time discussing in depth the foreign policy views that most evangelicals actually hold (such as their general support of torture of terrorist detainees, a point he even concedes), keeping in mind how allegedly credulous statements by more progressive evangelicals perhaps serve as an important corrective to the uncritical nationalism that has characterized much of evangelicalism in the US during the twentieth century. We get little discussion of the evangelical support of both laity and leaders for the second Iraq War or their general acquiescence to practices of "enhanced interrogation." And though progressive evangelical formal statements are labeled as naïve, Amstutz neglects the more pervasive geopolitical ignorance at work in evangelical international efforts like the hugely popular Kony 2012 viral internet phenomenon.

Another limitation of the book is Amstutz's restriction of the focus of the book to the work and thought of *United States* evangelicals. There is little consideration of the way that evangelicals outside of the U.S. have viewed, benefitted from, or been victimized by the foreign policy of this country. For example, how have Christians in Mexico interpreted US evangelical support for border control, or what is the character of Iraqi Christian understandings of US military involvement in their country? This obviously could be a result of the confines of space and scope. But perhaps it is a subtle reminder of how US evangelicals easily forget their ecclesial ties to brothers and sisters abroad due to enmeshment with their national identity or demands on the home front. One wonders what effect remembrance of these ties would have on US evangelicals, and how it might temper their nationalism or change the way they relate to other international communities for the better.

AARON GRIFFITH, *a member of Durham Mennonite Church and a doctoral student in American religious history at Duke Divinity School, Durham, NC.*

Kwok Pui-lan, *Globalization, Gender, and Peacebuilding: The Future of Interfaith Dialogue*, Paulist Press, 2012. 102 pp. $9.95. ISBN: 9780809147724.

In this compact study, Kwok Pui-lan, William F. Cole Professor of Christian Theology and Spirituality at the Episcopal Divinity School, offers an outline for a proposal for how to think about and practice interfaith dialogue in a globalized world in which violent conflicts are often constructed in religious terms. Originally presented as lectures at the University of Notre Dame, the chapters have a conversational quality, and footnotes are kept to a minimum. Some readers might be frustrated that Kwok gestures at some complicated matters (such as the implications of current debates within the religious studies field about how the modern category of religion has its roots within liberal Christian theology) while leaving them underdeveloped. However, Kwok's presentation has the salutary effect of being accessible to the non-specialist reader.

Kwok's direct, uncomplicated style arguably connects with one of her key claims, namely, that "interfaith dialogue must not be confined to narrow academic circles and among the elites if it is going to have a wider impact on faith communities and society" (3). Kwok in particular underscores a point made by Ursula King that "feminism is a missing dimension of interfaith dialogue" (31), noting how many academic and official, institutional forms of interfaith dialogue have excluded women's voices. Kwok correctly notes the dangers of some Western feminist approaches contributing to Islamophobia by portraying Islam in essentialist terms as anti-feminist, and cites Harvard scholar Leila Ahmed's work on women and Islam as a resource for countering such simplistic appraisals. Kwok's argument could have been extended and deepened by considering what implications the work of a scholar like Saba Mahmood (in *The Politics of Piety: The Islamic Revival and the Feminist Subject*) has for thinking about the implications of feminism for interfaith dialogue, specifically, the implications of Mahmood's argument that the women's mosque movement in Egypt embodies a form of agency focused on the cultivation of piety rather than on a secular-liberal form of feminist agency defined by the polarity of resistance and freedom. A theological engagement with Mahmood's work might have led Kwok to acknowledge more radical interfaith difference than her proposal sometimes seems to allow.

Kwok positions her argument against what has become a standard typology of theological approaches to religious diversity: that of exclusivism, inclusivism, and pluralism. Within this typology, Kwok's sympathies lie clearly with the pluralist camp. She favorably discusses the work of Diana Eck of Harvard's Pluralism Project and concurs with Eck's definition of pluralism as more than diversity and tolerance, but rather as "the energetic engagement with diversity," "the active seeking of understanding across lines of difference," and "the encounter of commitments" (14–15). Adding to pluralist discourse, Kwok builds on recent arguments for polydoxy, which Kwok describes as going "beyond the liberal claims that all religions are equally valid, for its asserts that we cannot know our own tradition without seeing it in relation to and through the lens offered by other religious and spiritual traditions" (77). Kwok also cites Colleen Hartung's definition of polydoxy as "a place of many faiths within a circle of faith" that "implies an openness to diversity, difference, challenge, and multiplicity" (69).

Kwok deploys postcolonial definitions of hybridity in her argument against exclusivism and inclusivism, both of which she views as trying to defend essentialist understandings of religion. Taking hybridity seriously, for Kwok, means taking seriously the internal diversity of supposedly closed totalities and means abandoning a search for a common core supposedly shared by all religions.

However, despite her best intentions, Kwok's account of polydoxy appears to succumb to the neo-colonial logic of inclusivism that she wishes to avoid. Her affirmation of Hartung's polydoxy as a "place of many faiths within a circle of faith" continues the inclusivist move of presenting religious diversity as either located within a common field or expressing a common core. In her argument against exclusivist preoccupations with boundary maintenance and defense, and with her essentialist accounts of religious difference, Kwok arguably errs in the other direction: that is, she does not take religious difference seriously enough.

ALAIN EPP WEAVER, *Mennonite Central Committee worker in Akron, PA, and is part of East Chestnut Street Mennonite Church in Lancaster, PA.*

News and Events

Vsit our website at www.anabaptistwitness.org!

On our website you can:

- Download PDF files of articles
- Read translation of Neal Blough's article
- Access online exclusives from Stuart Murray and Jacob Landis
- Find our blog, information about upcoming events, and other ways to connect with Anabaptist Witness

---

Up Coming Event : 2015 Shenk Mission Lectureship

Dates: April 17-18, 2015
Location: Anabaptist Mennonite Biblical Seminary, and
           Mennonite Church USA offices, Elkhart, IN

Mark your calendars!
Anabaptist Witness is pleased to announce the revival of the Shenk Mission Lectureship. Conference theme will be circulated in the coming weeks. Check our events page for more information (anabaptistwitness.org/events).

A Call for Papers
for the April 2015 issue of Anabaptist Witness:

Anabaptist Mission and Theology of Religions

Extended Submission Deadline: November 15, 2014

A new awareness of the diversity of global beliefs and practices has led to renewed attention to Christian theology of religions. This theology aims to articulate how Christians might understand and relate to persons and communities that do not share Christian faith. As such, theology of religions is related to conversations around religious pluralism, interfaith dialogue, and comparative religions.

In this issue of Anabaptist Witness, we invite contributions that put a theology of religions into conversation with reflection on Anabaptists and Mennonites in mission. What difference does a given theology of religions make to Anabaptists and Mennonites in mission? How might the realities of Anabaptists and Mennonites in mission shape a theology of religions? Contributions may focus on specific cultures and religions, as well as on general and theoretical issues. We also welcome historical treatments of how Anabaptists and Mennonites have, in word and deed, understood and responded to the diversity of human beliefs and practices in the past.

Because we hope for this journal to be an exchange among peoples from around the world, from laity and pastors to academics and administrators, Co-Editors welcome submissions from a variety of genres including sermons, photo-essays, reflections, interviews, biographies, poems, and academic papers.

For additional information on guidelines and deadlines, please visit out website: anabaptist.org/calls-for-submissions/

Address all correspondence to Anabaptist Witness Co-Editor, Jamie Pitts (jpitts@ambs.edu).

Anabaptist Witness is sponsored by Anabaptist Mennonite Biblical Seminary, Mennonite Church Canada, and Mennonite Mission Network.

32896037R00103

Made in the USA
Middletown, DE
22 June 2016